Henry Sutherland Edwards

Russian Projects Against India

From the Czar Peter to General Skobeleff

Henry Sutherland Edwards

Russian Projects Against India
From the Czar Peter to General Skobeleff

ISBN/EAN: 9783337168735

Printed in Europe, USA, Canada, Australia, Japan

Cover: Foto ©ninafisch / pixelio.de

More available books at **www.hansebooks.com**

RUSSIAN PROJECTS
AGAINST INDIA

FROM THE CZAR PETER
TO GENERAL SKOBELEFF

> "A knowledge of this region and its resources leads inevitably to the conclusion that our presence in Turkestan, in pursuance of Russian interests is justifiable solely on the ground of an endeavour to solve the Eastern question in our own favour from this quarter. Otherwise the hide is not worth the tanning and all the money sunk in Turkestan is lost."
>
> SKOBELEFF'S PROJECT FOR THE INVASION OF INDIA. PAGE 285.

BY

H SUTHERLAND EDWARDS

(WITH MAP)

LONDON
REMINGTON & CO PUBLISHERS
HENRIETTA STREET COVENT GARDEN
1885

[All Rights Reserved]

PREFACE.

THIS book has not, as the title and time of publication might suggest, been written under the impression of recent events in connection with the Afghan frontier. Much of it has already appeared in the form of articles, published from time to time in newspapers, magazines, and reviews during the last eight or nine years. These articles were all written with one object; that of showing that Russian expeditions in Central Asia (supported at critical moments by Russian intriguers in Persia and Afghanistan) have always been undertaken, not with a view to an improved frontier, the Russian frontier on the Central Asian side having never been threatened; nor for commercial purposes, the exports and imports between Russia and the Khanates being of the most trifling value, and quite out of proportion with the cost of occupying and administering the Russian possessions in Central Asia: but simply in order to place Russia in a position to threaten and, on a fitting opportunity, attack India. I have made no inferences. I have simply reproduced what the Russians themselves have avowed and proclaimed on the subject. In doing so I have drawn largely on the invaluable contributions to the history of Russian relations with Central Asia made by Mr. Robert Michell, of the India Office, whose unremitting study of the subject extends now over twenty years.

CONTENTS.

CHAP. PAGE

I. Expeditions towards India from the Reign of Peter the Great to that of Paul 1

II. Projects and Expeditions under Alexander I., Paul, and Nicholas 32

III. The First Russian Agent in Afghanistan... ... 63

IV. Perofski's Expedition 74

V. Perofski's Expedition *(continued)* 107

VI. Perofski's Expedition *(continued)* 124

VII. The Anglo-Russian Agreement of 1844 ... 149

VIII. Ignatieff's Mission to Khiva and Bokhara ... 157

IX. Ignatieff's Mission to Khiva and Bokhara *(continued)* 173

X. Kauffmann's Expedition to Khiva 212

XI. The Good and the Evil done by Russia in Central Asia 246

XII. Projects for the Invasion of India 260

been attacked, or at least approached by Russia through regular expeditions (not to speak of desultory attacks by Cossacks), no less than four times; and those who hold that in invading Khiva Russia had no aim in view but the extension of her possessions in Central Asia, will find their views contradicted somewhat flatly by Captain Mouravieff, in a striking passage from a work which that officer published 63 years ago.

As soon as the Settlement of Vienna in 1814 and 1815 left Russia free to divert her attention once more from European affairs and to direct it towards Central Asia, expeditions were at once equipped for service in the Steppes. Diplomatic missions, too, and commercial caravans, both under military escort, were sent to Khiva and to Bokhara. The chief emissary to Khiva was Captain Mouravieff; and on his return to Russia in 1822 he expressed, in a narrative of his journey, his deep regret that Russia had not yet succeeded in annexing the Khanate, whose capital he regarded as an invaluable stronghold from which to threaten the English power in India. "Khiva," he wrote, "is at this moment an advanced post which impedes our commerce with Bokhara and Northern India. Under our dependence

Khiva would have become a safeguard for this commerce against the attacks of populations dispersed in the Steppes of Southern Asia. This oasis, situated in the midst of an ocean of sand, would have become a point of assembly for all the commerce of Asia, and would have shaken to the centre of India the enormous superiority enjoyed by the rulers of the sea!"

In these lines Captain Mouravieff was only expressing what had been thought and felt by Russian politicians and Russian military commanders for a century and a half or a century and a quarter previously; nor, it need scarcely be added, have those thoughts and feelings been once abandoned during the last 50 or 60 years. Apart from such commercial importance as might or might not be claimed for it, Khiva, as we know from the published writings of Russian military commanders, was regarded as a post from which one of several converging forces might advantageously be directed against Merv, just as Merv used to be regarded as a post from which a march might be made upon Herat. But when the first Russian expedition against Khiva was sent out, no thought could have been entertained by the Russian Government of injuring England, which, like France, Portugal, Holland, and Denmark, had possessions in India, but was far, indeed, from exercising exclusive sway in that country. Peter the Great's sole object in connection with the East was to obtain for Russia a share of the riches for which that part of the world was famous. He wished to reach the country over which the English now rule. But Khiva and Bokhara were in his eyes nothing more than convenient stages towards the Oxus; and from the Oxus his emissaries were to make their way, not to any English possession, but to Delhi, at that time the capital of the Great Mogul.

A merchant known as Simon "Malinki," or Simon the Little, was the chief of Peter's envoys, and it is stated in the official *"Narrative of the Russian Military Expedition to Khiva, conducted by Prince Alexander Bekovitch Cherkaski, in* 1717," translated for the India Office by Mr. John Michell, that Simon died at Schmaikha on his way back; though in the official *"Narrative of the Russian Military Expedition to Khiva under Perofski in* 1839," translated from the Russian for the Foreign Department of the Government of India by Mr. Robert Michell, it is set forth that "Simon Malinki was despatched to

India in 1694, but died on his way thither at Schmaikha."

Whether Simon the Little did or did not reach India, it is certain that no information was derived from any report of his making; and when in 1716 the Russian Senate, at the command of Peter, ordered that an inquiry should be made as to the contents of the letter sent with the merchant Simon Malinki to the Mogul, and as to what it had led to, it appeared that the result, if any, of the merchant's journey had remained unknown.

Peter had now, in the year 1716, no idea of sending out a commercial or quasi-commercial mission alone. A Turcoman chief, Hodja Nefes by name, had come to him, saying that in the country bordering the river Amu (Oxus) gold sand was to be found, and that the stream, which formerly flowed into the Caspian, and which, through fear of the Russians, had been diverted by the Khivans into the Aral Lake, might, by destroying the dam, be made to run again in its original channel. Some years before an alliance had been proposed to Peter by the Khivan Khan, who even declared himself willing to become Peter's vassal. The Czar accepted the proffered allegiance; and when Hodja Nefes inflamed his avarice and his ambition by telling him of this river whose sands were gold, and along whose dried-up course he might reach the capital of his Khivan feudatory, he could not but entertain the project of a serious military expedition.

Peter was quite aware that Khiva and Bokhara were not commercial cities. "But," in the words of the official historian, "they were of great importance as channels of trade with other Asiatic countries, famous of old for the variety and abundance of their natural wealth." The visit of Hodja Nefes to St. Petersburg took place in 1713, just when Peter had finally defeated Charles XII. He had also brought his war against Turkey to a conclusion, and finding nothing to occupy him in the West, turned his attention, as his successors under like circumstances have systematically done, towards the East. He, perhaps, did not believe much in Hodja Nefes's tale of the gold to be found mingled with the sands of the Oxus. But he was struck by the story of the ancient bed, and entered warmly into the project of turning the Oxus into the channel along which it had at one time flowed. This would make it run into the Caspian Sea, and would bring the Caspian and Khiva into direct water communication.

Peter decided then to send an expedition against Khiva, and to do so in such a way that while the envoy should ostensibly be escorted only by a guard of honour numerous enough to give dignity to his mission, he should, in fact, be followed by an army sufficiently strong to overcome all resistance that might be opposed by the Khan.

Khivan towns had previously been attacked and occupied by Cossacks making war on their own account. But these minor expeditions had not been conducted with any system, nor had they been executed under the direction of the Russian Government. Peter's army of invasion, however, was to be regularly organised; and the object of its march was to bring Khiva into absolute subjection. "Although Khiva and Bokhara," in the words of the official historian, "were of themselves insignificant from their poverty in natural products and the undeveloped condition of their trade and industry, yet they were of extreme importance as channels of trade with other Asiatic countries famed of old for the variety and abundance of their natural wealth; so that the acquisition of Khiva as a first step must have been a point of great importance to the far-seeing Czar, more especially since he was assured of the possibility of turning the largest river of Central Asia into the Caspian, and of thus opening a convenient channel of communication even with remote confines of India."

So anxious was Peter to obtain information in respect to India that he had already invited Ashur Bek, the Khivan envoy at St. Petersburg, to undertake a mission to that country. Nothing, however, came of the proposition.

Having quite made up his mind to attack Khiva, Peter entrusted the command of the expedition to Prince Bekovitch Cherkaski, of the Body Guard, and ordered him in the first place, before adopting any military measures, to "congratulate the new Khan on his accession to power."

Prince Bekovitch made a preliminary reconnaissance and journey of exploration; after which he was able to report to the Czar that the Amu, or Oxus, river had in ancient times flowed into the Caspian Sea, and that he had discovered the old bed into which it was proposed to turn its course. Peter gave Prince Bekovitch full instructions as to the method of invading the Khanate of Khiva, and placed at his disposal a force of 4,000 regular infantry, 2,000 Cossacks, and 100 dragoons—troops who at that time acted indifferently on horseback and on foot. The Prince was ordered to approach Khiva in the character of a friendly envoy; the somewhat remarkable strength of his military escort being accounted for, as before set forth, by a polite desire on his part, and on the part of the Czar, his master, to give due importance to the mission on which he was engaged. On reaching Khiva the Prince was to call upon the Khan to submit formally to Russia, on condition of the sovereignty of the Khanate being continued in his family; and he was to guarantee the Khan's personal security—perhaps, also, his fidelity to Russia—by attaching to him a guard of Russians. Once established in Khiva, Prince Bekovitch was to despatch two trade caravans—one to the Khan of Bokhara, the other to the Mogul of India; the first with the object of persuading the Khan of Bokhara to acknowledge Russian supremacy; the second with the view of opening up a route along the river Oxus to India, where enquiries were to be made about the natural products and commodities of the country.

The second caravan was also to ascertain whether

there was not a more direct road from India to the Caspian, in which case it was to return by it, mapping both routes. The chosen envoy for India was Lieutenant Kojin, of the Russian Navy. Several naval officers and merchants were placed under his command, and he received special instructions from Peter himself in these words: " He is to go, when the Brigadier, Prince Cherkaski, shall be able to dispense with him, by water as far up the Amu-Daria [Oxus river] as possible (or by others which may fall into it), to India, in the guise of a merchant, the real business being the discovery of a water-way to India. II. To inquire secretly about the river, in case progress by water be forbidden. III. To return, if possible, by the same route, unless it be ascertained that there is another and more convenient way by water; the water-way as well as the land-route to be carefully observed and described in writing, and to be mapped. IV. To notice the merchandise, particularly aromatic herbs and other articles that are exported from India. V. To examine into, and write an account of, all other matters which, though not mentioned here, may concern the interests of the empire."

While due preparations were being made for subjecting first Khiva, and afterwards Bokhara, the Court of Embassies drew up credentials in the most approved form to the chiefs of the threatened Khanates and the distant Mogul.

The expedition was not to consist of soldiers alone. Besides 6,000 troops, it was to include upwards of 200 sailors, who were to take with them boats of different sizes. The flotilla was in the first place to carry over to Gurief, on the east coast of the Caspian, the infantry, a portion of the dragoons, the whole of the artillery (22 pieces), a year's provisions for the whole force, and the necessary implements for the construction of forts, with timber for huts. The Cossacks, with the other half of the squadron of dragoons, the caravan, the baggage train, and a certain number of dragoon horses were to proceed by land; advancing from Astrakhan through Gurief towards Khiva; while the larger detachment, starting from Krasnovodsk, on the east shore of the Caspian, was to follow the ancient bed of the river. The two columns were to effect a junction near the river, and make a combined attack upon Khiva. The plan of the attack was left to the discretion of the commander. But when the Khan had once been reduced to subjection and prevailed upon, no matter by what means, to acknowledge Russian supremacy, Prince Bekovitch Cherkaski was, in the words of Peter's decree, as written by himself, "to ask him for vessels and to send a merchant in them to India by the Amu-Daria, ordering the same to ascend the river as far as vessels can go, and thence to proceed to India, recording the rivers and lakes, and describing the way by land and water, and particularly the water-way to India by lake or river, returning from India the same way; or should the merchant hear in India of a still better road to the Caspian Sea, to come back by that, and to describe it in writing."

In addition to the two columns which, advancing from different points, were to converge on the banks of the Oxus, and march together against Khiva, an expedition on a smaller scale was sent out under Lieutenant Kojin, the so-called "Envoy for India," to Astrabad on the Persian shore of the Caspian. Here he was to request from the Governor of the province permission for an officer to pass through Persia to Bokhara with letters from the Khan.

The Governor of Astrabad would not allow the officer to pass through Persian territory, by reason, as Lieutenant Kojin affirmed, of an insurrection in that country. Prince Simonof who, Kojin having failed, was despatched to Astrabad to apply once more for permission to pass through Persia, had a very different tale to tell. He declared, in a report on the subject to Prince Bekovitch Cherkaski, that on Lieutenant Kojin's arrival in the harbour, the Governor of Astrabad had sent officers to meet him and to bring him with the chiefs of his expedition to the town. But Lieutenant Kojin, as Prince Simonof reported, neither went himself nor suffered the leading members of his mission to go to Astrabad. Prince Simonof, in a final accusation, charged Lieutenant Kojin with having made an attack on a herd of buffaloes grazing harmlessly near the sea-shore, and of having, after this exploit, put back forthwith to sea.

That Lieutenant Kojin did not do his best at Astrabad to procure permission for the Indian envoy to advance from Persia to Bokhara seems probable enough; for throughout the campaign against Khiva he showed himself ill-disposed towards Prince Bekovitch Cherkaski, the commander-in-chief. He was entrusted, nevertheless, with the leadership of the advanced guard. With the view of conciliating the threatened Khan and of throwing him off his guard, and also for the purpose of obtaining information about Khiva and its approaches, Kojin despatched messengers, bearing presents, and announcing his intention to visit Khiva on a mission from the Czar.

While Prince Bekovitch was still engaged in organising the main body of the expedition, news reached him from various sources that his advance would be resisted. But this information had no effect in checking his ardour. When complete, his forces consisted of 3,000 fighting men, who were accompanied by merchants, with their servants, and by camp-followers and servants, to the number of 1,000. The train included 600 guards, 200 camels, and several hundred horses. The force was assembled at Astrakhan; and the advanced guard was in the first place sent across the Caspian to Gurief, which had been chosen as the head-quarters of the army on the east coast of the Caspian. Bekovitch himself at the earliest opportunity sailed from Astrakhan to Gurief. Lieutenant Kojin, who, as chief of the advanced guard, should have preceded him, could not be induced even to accompany him. Declining to move from Astrakhan, he sent to St. Petersburg a report in which he accused the commander-in-chief of an intention "treacherously to deliver the Russian troops into the hands of barbarians." On receipt of this despatch he was summoned to St. Petersburg, where he was brought before a court-martial and subjected to a stringent examination. Thrown into prison, he would probably have been executed but for the news which in due time reached St. Petersburg of the fate Prince Bekovitch and his army had met with.

When Prince Bekovitch's entire force had arrived at Gurief it remained there for about a month, making preparations for the difficult advance across the Steppe. Bekovitch now heard bad news of various garrisons which he had left in forts erected on the eastern shores of the Caspian, and especially at Krasnovodsk. They had been much enfeebled by sickness; and as it was, moreover, very difficult to obtain the necessary supply of horses and camels for the march of all the men at his disposal, he determined to leave the Krasnovodsk contingent in its forts and to advance to Khiva at the head of a single column. The column from Krasnovodsk was to have made its way along the dried-up bed of the Oxus. But it was now arranged to abandon altogether this interesting route.

Bekovitch's first encounter with the enemy took place while his force was still encamped at Gurief. He was attacked by Karakalpaks, who captured a portion of his cattle, and at the same time carried off 60 Cossacks under whose guard they had been placed. Bekovitch followed the Karakalpaks into the Steppe, recovered the oxen and brought back six of the assailants.

When all the necessary preparations had been made, the troops left Gurief at the beginning of June; in the worst possible season, that is to say, for campaigning in the Steppe. After eight days' marching, during which he met with several small streams, Prince Bekovitch Cherkaski reached the Emba, where, before attempting the passage, he was obliged to halt. The soldiers forded the river, while baggage was sent over on rafts; and the passage altogether occupied two days. From Gurief to the Emba the troops had marched 25 miles a day; they had thus accomplished a distance of about 200 miles. The commander had hastened his advance, partly lest the grass in the Steppe should be burnt up by the intense heat, partly with the view of reaching Khiva before the Khan would have time to collect any considerable number of troops for the defence of his capital. The Khan, however, was destined to receive early news of Bekovitch's progress; for, at two days' march from the Emba, a certain number of Turcomans and Kalmuks belonging to the expedition deserted and hurried on to Khiva in order to warn the Khan. Arrived within eight days of Khiva, the Russian commander sent on a messenger with an escort of Cossacks, bearing a letter in which the Khan was assured of Russia's peaceful intentions. The Prince wished simply to pay a visit to the Khan on behalf of his master the Czar; and that he might do so in a becoming style, he had caused himself to be accompanied by a numerous retinue. Continuing his march, Bekovitch met two days afterwards his messenger returning with two Khivans. Although the Prince had assured the Khan that he was advancing simply in the character of a friendly envoy, he nevertheless thought it advisable to make the two Khivans believe that the force under his command was composed of a far greater number of men than were really included in it. The strength of the column had been much reduced by forced marches; and numbers of stragglers and tired horses had been left behind. Under these circumstances it was thought desirable to inform the Khivan envoys that the main body of the army was nothing more than the advanced guard. Prince Bekovitch, it was added, was with the principal body of the army in the rear. They were made to wait two days; after which Bekovitch, who was supposed to have hurried on from his place at the head of the great bulk of the troops, received them in an audience. The Khivan messengers had brought with them as presents to the Russian general a horse, a *kaftan*, and a supply of fresh fruit and vegetables. Bekovitch informed them, as he had already informed their sovereign, that he was not going to Khiva with any hostile intentions, but simply as the ambassador of a friendly power and with the view of paying his respects to the Khan. His embassy, he admitted, had a political object but he reserved for himself the honour of communicating this to the Khan personally.

"Bekovitch's force," writes the official historian, "had marched from Gurief to the river Emba (200 miles) in 10 days; from the Emba to the Irket Hills (on the northern margin of the Ust-Urt—about 100 miles) in five days; 553 miles of a hilly country were next performed in 49 days. Descending the hills in two forced marches (67 miles in two days) the column emerged upon the arms or overflows of the Oxus, within 100 miles of Khiva, and encamped there on the 15th of August, 1717. The column consequently traversed in 65 days, or in about two months 900 miles of a barren and arid Steppe; and that, too, at the hottest time of the year. Throughout almost the whole length of the march the water obtained was of bad quality; at every halt wells were dug to a depth of from two to four fathoms. From this alone the sufferings of the troops (in a heat which sometimes exceeded 40° Réaumur) may well be imagined."

The Khan showed himself as great an adept as Prince Bekovitch himself at the noble game of brag. He seems in the first instance to have been well disposed towards the Russians, and to have believed in their assurances of friendship. When, however, the Kalmuk and Turcoman deserters reached Khiva, he could no longer make any mistake as to the purpose of Bekovitch's advance. He summoned troops from every side, and industriously circulated the report that he was about to take the command of 100,000 men, when, as a matter of fact, he was not able to assemble more than 24,000. Hearing that the

Khan was marching to attack him, Bekovitch resolved to fight a defensive battle, and drew up his troops with their rear to the river bank, and with their flanks and front covered by barricades of carts. Scarcely had he completed these preparations when the Khivan cavalry made its appearance, and at once swept down upon the camp. At night the Khivans retired some distance, "sitting down before the Russians, and enclosing them in the form of a crescent." Bekovitch meanwhile dug a trench and erected earthworks, which he fortified with six guns—all the artillery that he had been able to bring forward; so that when, next morning, the attack was renewed, the Russians were well prepared to meet it. The whole of that day and the day following the fight was kept up, when the Khivans, finding that their onslaught produced no effect, determined to have recourse to negotiations.

The charge of the Khivan cavalry had done but little injury to the well-protected Russians, and their fire-arms of primitive make had killed but 10 of the enemy. The Khivans however, had suffered greatly from the Russian musketry and artillery fire.

When, on the morning of the fourth day, an envoy arrived from the Khan begging Prince Bekovitch to grant him an audience, the messenger began by declaring that the attack had been made without the knowledge of the Khan, who had only just arrived, and who had never intended that the Russians should be in any way molested. If Prince Bekovitch, he continued, had come to Khiva as a friendly envoy, he would be well received. The messenger requested that some one belonging to the Russian force might be permitted to return with him to the Khan, so as to give an authentic reply to his sovereign's words; and Bekovitch sent a Tartar, who was instructed to inform the Khan in his own language that the Prince "was the bearer of credentials and of verbal communications from the Czar." After being received by the Khan, the Tartar messenger came back to the Russian force, saying that the Khan meant to hold a council that day, and that the day afterwards he would send a formal communication; meanwhile all fighting was to be considered at an end.

Bekovitch, on his side, held a council, at which it was determined not to refuse offers of peace if they seemed advantageous; though several of the officers, with Major Frankenberg at their head, opposed this view. It was necessary, however, to count with circumstances. The troops had undergone much fatigue, and it was impossible within the entrenched camp to find pasture for the horses and camels. While Bekovitch and his officers were still deliberating, the Khivans renewed the attack. Bekovitch replied to the onslaught, but at the same time sent the Tartar messenger to inform the Khan of what was taking place, and to remonstrate with him on the subject. The Khan recalled the troops, and declared that, as on a previous occasion, the offenders had acted without his knowledge and against his wish, and that they were not Khivan troops but Turcomans and tribes from the Aral sea. By way of proving to Bekovitch that the attack had been made without his authority the Khan ordered two Khivans, who were accused of having instigated it to be punished before Bekovitch's messengers in the following manner:—They were to be "led in front of the whole army by a thin string drawn through the nostril of the one, and the ear of the other."

To this droll penalty the culprits were, in fact, subjected. Then two of the Khivan ministers proceeded to the Russian camp, where a preliminary treaty was arranged, and sworn to on both sides; the Khan's ministers kissing the Koran, and Prince Bekovitch the cross. The day following Prince

Bekovitch paid a visit to the Khan, attended by his principal officers, his brothers, and a detatchment of Cossacks and dragoons, to the number of 700. Bekovitch exhibited his credentials, and delivered the presents he bore from the Emperor, consisting of "cloth, sugar, skins of sable, nine dishes, nine plates, and nine silver spoons." The Khan ratified the treaty, made personal protestations of friendship, and invited the Russian commander and his officers to a dinner, which, says the official historian, was "enlivened by the strains of the Russian military band."

The day after the interview and banquet the Khan, with his entire army, and accompanied by Prince Bekovitch and his principal officers as honoured guests, marched to Khiva. The cautious Major Frankenberg, who mistrusted the Khivans *et dona ferentes,* had been left in command of the Russian troops, with orders to follow the Khan and the Khivan army as rapidly as might be convenient. He probably believed, what afterwards proved to be the case, that at the council held after the four days' attack upon the Russian entrenched camp, the Khan had devised a plan for disposing of the Russians in detail, without meeting the army in the field.

However this may have been, Bekovitch, on arriving at Khiva, was told that it would be impossible to feed and quarter the Russians in that city; and he was accordingly invited to separate his own escort, and the Russian army generally, into a number of small parties, so that accommodation might be found for them in the towns adjoining the capital. The sagacious Major Frankenberg, when Bekovitch directed him to break up his force into a number of little detachments, protested against doing anything of the kind. He replied to the messenger who bore the order that this was an idea of the Khan's, and that it was his duty to obey the orders of Prince Bekovitch, the commander of the Russian troops. Although inspired by the Khan, the order had really proceeded from Bekovitch; but he was obliged to repeat it twice, and still could not make the determined Major act upon it. At last the Prince despatched a fourth written order, threatening Frankenberg with a court-martial if he refused any longer to do his duty. Then the acting commander-in-chief divided his force into five different detachments, which were conducted by the Khivans in various directions. This break-up of the Russian force was all that the Khan had desired. Prince Bekovitch had no sooner sent away his own private escort than he was made prisoner and killed, while his brothers and brother officers were either cut down on the spot, or stripped naked to be hacked to pieces at leisure. The comparatively small parties of Russian troops, numbering each at the utmost from 200 to 300 men, were set upon and massacred; and the Khan then entered in triumph his city of Khiva, where he exposed on a gibbet the heads of two Russian princes belonging to Cherkaski's escort, stuffed with hay. The head of Cherkaski himself was forwarded as a gift to the Khan of Bokhara; who returned it with expressions of disgust, and with an inquiry whether the Khan of Khiva was a cannibal?

It was not until September, 1717, that news of the terrible fate encountered by Prince Cherkaski's expedition reached the occupants of the forts on the eastern coast of the Caspian. A report on the subject was at once transmitted to the Czar.

The catastrophe did not unduly affect the dauntless Peter, who, far from abandoning his views in respect to Central Asia, gave orders for the regiments at the stations on the east coast of the Caspian to be at once raised to their full complement. But the garrisons were so much enfeebled, and they were exposed to such fierce attacks from the Turcoman tribes, that their chiefs, in spite of the orders they had received from St. Petersburg, thought it advisable to embark with them for Astrakhan. The 13 vessels in which they sailed were dispersed in a storm and for the most part wrecked. No less than 400 of the returning troops were lost. The rest contrived to reach the shore—still the eastern shore of the Caspian; where they had great difficulty in finding means of subsistence. In the spring, however, of the following year, those who had not succumbed were picked up by vessels sent in search of them, and carried to Astrakhan.

Thus ended the ill-fated expedition of Prince Bekovitch Cherkaski, which, after rapid marching and energetic fighting, was destroyed through an act of treachery against which its commander ought certainly to have been on his guard. It was pleaded on his behalf that he had recently suffered great misfortunes, that he had been sorely tried during the brief but arduous campaign, and that his mind was to some extent unhinged. He received, in fact, when on the point of marching from Gurief, news that his wife and a portion of his family had been wrecked and drowned in the Caspian Sea. He seems, nevertheless, to have been in full possession of his nerve during the prolonged attack on the Russian camp. His expedition was, in any case, attended with the most tragic results; and it has been seen that even the small column left behind at Krasnovodsk, on the east coast of the Caspian, was destined to meet with a like fate to that reserved for the column which had advanced.

The disaster caused a great impression in Russia, when "to perish like Bekovitch" became a proverbial phrase for expressing utter annihilation.

For the next 14 years Russia left Khiva alone; though, even from an earlier period than the reign of Peter, the Czars had made endeavours to strengthen their influence in Khiva on every suitable occasion. "From the time of John the Terrible," to quote the official historian of Perofski's expedition, "the Russians have always sought means for opening a channel for their trade through Central Asia with India, in order to acquire some of that fabulous wealth for which India was always so celebrated." Peter, however, was the first Russian sovereign to send out a regular expedition against Khiva— the ill-fated expedition led by Prince Bekovitch in 1717.

Peter again thought of Khiva in 1731. But this time he contented himself with sending a simple negotiator in the person of Colonel Herzenberg. Herzenberg, however, was not allowed to enter the capital; and in addition to this insult he had to submit to the injury of being plundered on his homeward journey.

In the year 1741 Abdul Khair, Khan of the Lesser Horde, and a friend of the Russians, having had the throne of Khiva offered to him by Nadir Shah, who had caused the late sovereign to be put to death, Lieutenant Gladysheff, of the Russian army, the Russian surveyor Mouravin, and the Russian engineer, Nazimoff, entered Khiva in company with the new prince. But the interference of the Russians led to nothing. Mouravin visited Nadir Shah in his camp to request "that he, Nadir Shah, would give up the town of Khiva for the sake of His Imperial Highness Abdul Khair, for that the latter was a good and faithful subject of the Russian Empire." Nadir made presents to the envoy, and accepted his proposals. But he at the same time requested Abdul Khair to seek a personal interview with him; and the latter considered this invitation so alarming that he left Khiva in haste, the Russian officers, who apparently shared his views, accompanying him. In due time, and after a brief occupation by Nadir Shah, the throne of Khiva was offered to and accepted by Khan Nour Ali, Abdul Khair's son.

The Empress Catherine was so much occupied with Western affairs, and especially with intrigues in Poland and wars in the Balkan peninsula, that she had no time to bestow on Central Asian politics. Nevertheless, when in 1793 the Khan of Khiva requested the Empress to send him a physician to cure his uncle Fazil of ophthalmia, Her Majesty at once consented, and despatched an observant oculist named Blankenagel. Arriving at Khiva, the conscientious doctor declared the eyes of the patient to be incurable. This irritated the Khan, and when Blankenagel proposed at once to return, he found himself detained until a Khivan council could come to a determination as to how he was to be dealt with. A powerful majority of notabilities recommended that he should be allowed to start, and put to death on the road. This proposition was formally adopted. But Blankenagel was informed by some Russians in captivity at Khiva of what awaited him in case of his remaining, and he succeeded in making his escape. He in the first place took refuge with a Turcoman tribe, and afterwards, through their aid, reached Mangishlak, on the east coast of the Caspian, whence he sailed to Astrakhan. Arrived in St. Petersburg, Blankenagel wrote a description of his visit to Khiva, and in one passage of the work laid great stress on the possibility, as it seemed to him, of uniting the Aral Lake with the Caspian Sea by turning the waters of the Oxus into its ancient bed; a project, as is generally known to all who pay the slightest attention to the affairs of Central Asia, which has occupied the Russians from the time of Peter I. until that of Alexander II., and which, on the occasion of an overflow of the Oxus, was revived with considerable energy only the other day.

Blankenagel entertained a quite unfounded opinion of the wealth of Khiva. "I have shown," he wrote, "what assurances I gathered regarding the rich and inexhaustible gold and silver mines of Khiva. These great treasures will cost us much less in respect of working and carriage than those of Peru cost Spain." In regard to the commercial as distinguished from the industrial question, he expressed himself as follows: "All these rich branches of trade depend on the possession of Khiva, and ought to be so much more important to us, in that, to acquire this new Peru, it is not necessary to arm fleets, despatch large bodies of troops, or expend much blood and treasure. In a word, the possession of Khiva will cost us nothing, and this nothing will procure for Russia great wealth, and what is more pleasing tranquillity and peace for the natives. . . . I venture to say in all confidence that 5,000 men could without difficulty occupy the whole of the Khivan territory."

No other expedition or mission, military, commercial, scientific, or benevolent, was despatched to Khiva until the reign of Paul; when one of the strangest marches ever conceived was not only resolved upon, but in part executed, by one of the Orloffs. The enterprising chief, at the head of a force composed entirely of Cossacks and horse artillery, proposed to advance, first to Khiva, then to Bokhara, and ultimately, with all the adventurous horsemen of the Steppes who could be induced to join, to India itself!

CHAPTER II.

PROJECTS AND EXPEDITIONS UNDER ALEXANDER I., PAUL, AND NICHOLAS.

IT has been seen that besides sending independent commercial missions to India, Peter the Great, in connection with Prince Bekovitch's ill-fated expedition, despatched officers who were to make their way to India in the character and costume of merchants. His successors, too, following out his instructions and views, aimed at establishing themselves in Central Asia; thus, in the words of an official writer, "to open a new route for Russian commerce in the East." But the first Russian sovereign who conceived the idea of sending troops to India for the express purpose of injuring England and of destroying her dominion in Hindostan was the Emperor Paul; who, though slightly crazy, possessed a considerable amount of political insight.

In arranging his attack on the English settlements in India, the Emperor Paul sought the co-operation of Napoleon; and the French Emperor seemed disposed at one time to join in Paul's project, which, referring to it at St. Helena, he declared to be far from impracticable.

Paul, in fact, proposed nothing more than what Nadir Shah not long before had really accomplished. Indeed, a whole series of Tartar conquerors had marched from Central Asia through Afghanistan into India; and it seemed to Paul and to Orloff, whom he entrusted with the command of his expedition against the English in India, that, after making his way to Khiva, as Bekovitch had done, an enterprising chief might raise the Turcoman tribes as he advanced, and, accompanied by these plunder-loving nomads, go on from Khiva to Bokhara, and from Bokhara to India; where it was proposed that the unhappy English should be "driven from their settlements on the Indus." This attempt was to be made without any risk on the part of Russia beyond the possible sacrifice of a few regiments of Cossacks.

Paul, however, had two plans for attacking the English in India. Anticipating Russian strategists of a later period, he proposed to make his way to Afghanistan, at one time through Persia or along the Persian frontier by the road to Herat and Candahar; at another through the Khanates of Khiva and Bokhara. His first plan was to march from Astrabad by the road to Herat and Candahar; and in a despatch to Napoleon on the subject, he proposed that, with a combined army of 70,000 men, France and Russia should "chase the English from India, liberate that rich and beautiful country from the English yoke, and open new roads to England's commercial rivals, and especially to France." Paul was by no means solicitous of confining to France and Russia the honour and advantage of expelling the English from India; and in a memorandum on the subject (cited a few years ago by the St. Petersburg *Vedomosti*) he considered in the first place "what Powers should be invited to take part in the project of a march to India."

"The French Republic," he wrote, "and the Emperor of Russia must send a combined force of 70,000 men to the borders of India. But the Emperor of Germany (*i.e.*, Austria) must also join; for it would be necessary to have his permission for the French army to pass through his territory, and sail down the

Danube. . . . As soon as the plan has been perfectly matured," continued Paul, "the Russian Emperor will give orders for the assembling at Astrakhan of an army of 35,000 men—25,000 regular troops of all arms, and 10,000 Cossacks. Astrabad will be the headquarters of the combined army. From the Danube to the borders of India the advance will occupy the French army four months, or, avoiding forced marches, five months. The armies to be preceded by commissaries, who will establish stations and halting-places where necessary. They will visit, moreover, the khans and great landowners through whose countries the troops will pass, in order to explain that the armies of two powerful nations have found it necessary to march by a road which is being prepared to India for the purpose of driving away the English from this beautiful country which they have subjected; a country formerly so remarkable for its industry and wealth, and which it is now proposed to open to all the world, that the inhabitants may profit by the riches and other advantages given to them by heaven. The sufferings under which the population of this country groans have inspired France and Russia with the liveliest interest; and the two Governments have resolved to unite their forces in order to liberate India from the tyrannical and barbarous yoke of the English. Accordingly, the princes and populations of all countries through which the combined armies will pass need fear nothing. On the contrary, it behoves them to help with all their strength and means so benevolent and glorious an undertaking; the object of this campaign being in all respects as just as was unjust the campaign of Alexander the Great, who wished to conquer the whole world. The commissaries are further to set forth that the combined armies will not levy contributions, and will pay in ready money, on terms freely agreed to, for all things necessary to their sustenance: that on this point the strictest rules will be enforced. Moreover, that religion, laws, manners, and customs, property and women, will everywhere be respected and protected. With such announcements, with such honest, straightforward statements, it is not to be doubted that the khans and other small princes will allow the combined armies to pass without hindrance through their territories. In any case they are too weak and too much divided by dissensions among themselves to make any opposition. The commissaries will hold negotiations with the khans, princes, and private landowners about furnishing provisions, carts, and kibitkas. They will subscribe conditions, and according to circumstances will require, or themselves deposit, caution-money. Learned and artistic societies must take part in the glorious expedition. Aeronauts and pyrotechnists will be of the highest value; and to inspire the population with a high idea of France and Russia, it will be arranged, before the army starts from Astrabad, to hold grand fêtes and perform striking evolutions in the style of those with which great events and memorable epochs are celebrated at Paris."

"How," asked Napoleon in reply, "when the combined army has reached Astrabad, will it penetrate to India, across a barren and almost savage country, a distance of 300 leagues?"

"The country," answered the Emperor Paul, "is not savage; it is not barren. It has long been traversed by open and spacious roads. The soil is like that of Arabia and Libya—not covered with dry sand. Rivers water it at almost every step. There is no want of grass for fodder. Rice grows in abundance and forms the principal food of the inhabitants."

Strangely enough, General Khruleff, recommending fifty-seven years afterwards just such an advance against India as the Emperor Paul, in his memorandum to Napoleon on the subject, had proposed, repeated what the Emperor Paul had set forth as to the fertility of the country between the Caspian and Herat. General Khruleff would scarcely have trusted for his facts to such a visionary as Paul; and probably both the Emperor Paul and General Khruleff borrowed their information from some official report preserved in the Russian achives. "The grazing land," wrote General Khruleff at the time of the Crimean war, "is good; and water, rice, barley, and sheep are procurable in plenty."

The alliance, however, between France and Russia came to an end, and all idea of a Russo-French expedition to India was lost sight of. But Paul did not abandon his project. He resolved to execute it without the aid of the French, and, instead of the road to Herat and Candahar, to adopt the Khiva-Bokhara route. In the year 1801 General Orloff, Hetman of the Don, was sent with a force of Cossacks and horse artillery from the Don to Orenburg, and from Orenburg towards Khiva where on his arrival he was to organise, as best he could, an expedition to India. The plan of campaign was drawn up, and the motives for undertaking it explained in a rescript which first appeared in the appendix to General Miliutin's "*History of Souvaroff's Campaigns*" published in 1853, and brought out a few years afterwards in a German translation.

"The English," wrote Paul, "are preparing to attack me and my allies, the Swedes and Danes, by sea and by land. I am ready to receive them. But it is necessary also to attack them where the blow will be most felt, and where it is least expected. You will therefore proceed to India. From Orenburg three months, from your own part of Russia another month —altogether four months. I entrust this expedition entirely to you and your army. Collect your troops in the furthermost stations and await orders to march to Orenburg, where again expect orders to continue your march. This enterprise will cover you with glory, and according to your deserts, you will earn my special good-will. You will acquire riches and treasures, and will affright the enemy in his heart. I send you maps—as many as I have—and remain, your well-wisher, PAUL.

"P.S.—My maps only go as far as Khiva and the river Amu (Oxus). Beyond these points it is your affair to gain information about the possessions of the English, and the condition of the Indian populations subject to their rule." The following instructions are then given to Orloff:—" India, your destination, is governed by one chief ruler and a great many small ones. The English have, in this country, commercial establishments—which they acquired either with money or by arms. Our object is to destroy all these, to raise up the small rulers, and bring the land into the same dependence on Russia in which it now stands towards England."

Orloff is further told, in the name of his "well-wisher, Paul," and apparently by one of Paul's secretaries, that his despatch of the 25th of January has been received, and that its contents are approved, and require, therefore, no comment. Then in his own hand (as before) the Czar continues, under date of February 21st: " Take as many men as you can. As to infantry I am of your opinion, that you had better do without it."

Orloff marched from Orenburg in winter with 22,000 Cossacks and 44,000 horses, and with two companies of horse artillery ; and in rather less than a month traversed 685 versts—upwards of 450 miles. He had now reached the heights of Irgiz to the north of the Aral Lake; but he was to proceed no further. A despatch reached him announcing the death of Paul; and he at the same time received an order commanding him, on behalf of the new Emperor, Alexander I., to give up his enterprise and return forthwith to Russia.

Since the time of Paul, who, as above shown, formed two separate projects for invading India and " driving the English from their settlements on the Indus," every Russian emperor has entertained plans, or at least had plans submitted to him, either for invading India in a direct manner with Russian troops, or for destroying our position in that country by indirect means and chiefly through the agency of the Afghans. The first of Paul's projects was taken up by Alexander I.; or rather was pressed upon the acceptance of that sovereign by the Emperor Napoleon. Alexander agreed to co-operate in a combined Franco-Russian expedition, which was to march to India through Persia and Afghanistan. Nor was the idea abandoned until the two emperors fell out; when Napoleon prepared, not for an expedition with Russia to India, but for an expedition supported by troops from all parts of continental Europe against Russia.

In 1837 the Emperor Nicholas despatched an agent, Lieutenant Vitkievitch, to the Ameer of Cabul with propositions of support in arms, ammunition, and money against England's ally, Runjeet Singh ; and finally, in 1878, Alexander II. sent General Stolietoff to Cabul in order, as the Tashkend correspondent of the *Russian World* wrote at the time, " to establish direct commercial relations with Afghanistan and India."

Indeed since the reign of Peter the Great the Russian emperors, following the example of that sovereign, have never found themselves free from European complications but they have at once turned their attention towards Central Asia. A general settlement, so far as the West was concerned, having been effected in 1815, the Russian Government lost but little time before occupying itself once more with the affairs of Khiva and Bokhara ; and in 1819 formal instructions were given to General Yermoloff, commanding the army of the Caucasus, to Captain Mouravieff, of the General Staff, and Major Ponomareff, to reconnoitre the eastern shores of the Caspian, with the view of selecting a suitable spot for the construction of a fort with a warehouse for goods, and afterwards to proceed to Khiva, where the Khan was to be persuaded to direct the trade of his dominions towards the spot fortified. The two officers reconnoitred all the southern portion of the eastern shores of the Caspian, and found two points suitable for the erection of a fort, one near the mouth of the Gurgen, the other on the Balkan Gulf. The Yomood Turcomans inhabiting the shores not only refrained from annoying the Russian agents in the execution of their duty, but even asked to be taken under Russian protection. Escorted by a few Turcomans of this tribe, Mouravieff proceeded to Khiva without let or hindrance. But there he was thrown into prison and confined for a space of forty-eight days; and, although he eventually had an interview with the Khan, he failed in persuading him to adopt the propositions of his Government, and soon afterwards hurried away.

On his return Mouravieff described his travels, and represented in the most vivid colours the wretched condition of the Khanate; depicting, moreover, in sombre hues, the painful situation of the Russian captives.

More important than anything seen by Captain Mouravieff in Khiva is what he wrote on the subject after his return to Russia. "Khiva," he said (in a passage previously quoted, but which may be here reproduced) "is at this moment an advanced post which impedes our commerce with Bokhara and with Northern India. Under our dependence, Khiva would have been a safeguard for this commerce against the attacks of populations dispersed in the steppes of Southern Asia. This oasis, situated in the midst of an ocean of sand, would have become a point of assembly for all the commerce of Asia, and would have shaken to the centre of India the enormous superiority of the rulers of the sea."

Mouravieff's narrative is also remarkable as containing a denial of the favourite Russian belief (the "great Slavonian sea-serpent," as Kiepert, the German geographer, has called it) as to the diversion of the Oxus by the Khivans and the possibility of turning it back into its ancient bed. Whenever an expedition to Khiva has been planned—from the unfortunate one of Prince Bekovitch in the reign of Peter the Great, to the highly successful one of General Kaufmann under Alexander II.—the possibility of restoring the Oxus to its ancient bed has always been considered. When, some five-and-twenty years after Dr. Blankenagel, Captain Mouravieff visited Khiva, he recognised the fact—which no one now disputes—that the Oxus had at one time flowed into the Caspian. But he declined to entertain the idea that the stream had been diverted towards the Aral Lake, which now receives it, by the Khivans. "It is probable," he wrote, "that the river Syr (Jaxartes) was connected formerly with the Amu Daria (Oxus), or, at least, had a different course from that which it now follows. An earthquake, changing the entire horizon of the steppes, would seem to have given quite another direction to the Syr, which, with the Amu, forms the Aral Lake. Ancient historians say that the trade of India passed along the Oxus, which at that time threw itself into the Caspian Sea. The obscurity which surrounds the history of Central Asia, above all at the period of the destruction of the two great empires, has concealed great natural revolutions which changed the face of a portion of the steppe with which these regions are covered. The traces of these revolutions are still visible, and are above all recognisable in the new course of the Oxus and in its ancient bed.

"The very existence of that river has often been denied, and the belief in its non-existence acquired a certain consistency when the expedition sent by Peter the Great in search of the gold sand which was said to lie on its shores had failed disastrously. Prince Bekovitch, sent with a detachment to Khiva, built fortifications on the Krasnovodsk promontory, and proceeding to the northern shore of Balkan Bay, a hundred versts to the east, found the outlet of the river. He ascended its dried-up bed, but after a march of five versts, lost all traces of it. Captain Kojin, who was attached to the Prince, accused him of treason, and maintained that Bekovitch had only proclaimed the existence of the river with the view of delivering up his detachment to the Khan of Khiva. The year following, in 1717, Bekovitch went once more in search of the dam which the Khivans were supposed to have constructed with the view of directing the course of the river to the north, so as to protect themselves against the incursions of Cossacks."

"Bekovitch," continues Mouravieff, "perished in the second attempt, and his sad end caused all further curiosity as to the course of the Oxus to cease. If the Government proposed at this time to establish commercial relations with India by means of the Oxus, after making it flow once more into

Balkan Bay, it must be presumed that it had some idea of the vastness of this river. If so, how could it suppose that the barbarous Khivans could have been capable of turning the course of such a river by constructing a dam, and of changing the inclination of the steppe in order to direct the river towards the north. The Khivans themselves," he concludes, "are astonished at such a supposition. They have preserved traditions, according to which a violent earthquake five hundred years ago convulsed the whole surface of the country, and caused the Amu Daria to flow towards the north, and in its course to form for itself a new bed."

In 1820, in order on the one hand to support Russian authority, and on the other to render the passage of caravans secure, another mode of action was adopted. It was resolved to send yearly into the steppes detachments of a strength varying according to circumstances. But matters, instead of becoming better, became worse. In 1822 many Turcoman tribes acknowledged the authority of the Khan. War and rapine raged between the Russian Kirghizes and those who were still independent. The kidnapping of Russians from the frontier increased tenfold; piracy on the Caspian moreover took serious proportions, and inflicted great injury on Russian fishermen.

The Russian caravans, escorted by considerable detachments, were pillaged as before. Thus, in 1824, a caravan under the protection of a detachment consisting of 625 men and two guns, was attacked at the passage of the Yani river by hostile Kirghizes, reinforced by Khivans. For three days running the caravan defended itself, but finally had to throw away its merchandise and retire, with a loss of something like half a million roubles.

The kidnapping of Russians on the frontier did not cease. Every year some 200 Russians were captured on the Caspian and sold in the Khivan market. A special fund was held in trust on the frontier for their ransom.

In the year 1826, Colonel Berg having been sent with a detachment to make a survey of the territory between the Caspian and Aral seas, a report was spread that the Russians were preparing to send a new expedition to Khiva. A Khivan envoy was therefore sent to one of the forts on the Aral, taking with him an elephant as a present to the Emperor of Russia. The envoy, however, was informed that he would be allowed to proceed to St. Petersburg only on two conditions : first, that the Khan of Khiva should indemnify the Russian traders for all the losses they had sustained by the attack on their caravan in 1824; and, secondly, that all the Russian prisoners detained in Khiva should be sent back, and that all traffic in slaves should for the future be prohibited. These conditions were not agreed to by the Khan, and the envoy was sent back to Khiva.

At the beginning of 1830, things looking quiet and the Khivans, moreover, being nearly at war with Bokhara, the Russian Government thought the moment opportune for sending a new expedition to Khiva. An envoy from Bokhara had reached Orenburg with instructions to ask the Emperor of Russia to "put a limit to the insolent conduct of Khiva," and to offer the co-operation of the Emir, his master. The dissensions between the governments of Khiva and Bokhara had not yet taken the form of open hostilities; but the Bokharians at Orenburg declared positively that their Emir, even if he did not give active assistance to the Russians, would, at all events, be glad to see their common enemy restrained and punished. Khiva, too, was at this moment engaged in open war with Persia. Animosity, more-

E

over, existed between the Khivans and some of the Kirghiz chiefs. Thus Khiva was in a very critical position, and everything seemed to promise success to the Russian expedition which it was now determined to organize. But the French insurrection of July in this year seemed likely to disturb the peace of Europe ; and it was in fact followed by a formidable insurrection in Poland, which occupied the whole energies of the Russian Government, and caused all idea of conquest in Central Asia to be abandoned.

In 1830 the position of the Russians detained in Khiva was, according to an official report on the subject, as follows :—" Incited by the high prices fetched by Russians, the Kirghizes kidnapped them even on the line, and disposed of them in the neighbouring countries of Central Asia; particularly at Khiva, where according to reliable information, there were more than 2,000 Russians in bondage. In remote times men were seized from settlements in the interior, even on the Volga, and beyond that river, and subsequently on the Orenburg line. But about the year 1831 Russian fishermen alone were kidnapped by Kirghizes and Turcomans at the rate of about 200 every year. Russian prisoners were sold at the Khivan bazaars; and the traffic was participated in, not only by the highest Khivan officials, but likewise by Khivan traders who visited Russia every year, and who, when frequenting the Kirghiz encampments for purposes of trade, incited the Kirghizes to make prisoners, buying them up beforehand and giving money in advance. Although the Orenburg Frontier Commission had at its disposal a sum of 3,000 roubles for the redemption of Russian prisoners, it was only able to procure the liberation of a very small number, as sentence of death was awarded at Khiva to anyone who consented to sell his slave in order that he might be restored to his native country."

The Khivans, meanwhile, finding that the Russians, from whom they had expected an immediate attack, made no movement in their direction, became emboldened, and carried on to a greater extent than ever their practice of kidnapping. The idea was now entertained of seizing the Khivan traders visiting Russia, and keeping them as hostages. But this, it was thought, would have a very injurious effect on Central Asian trade; and all the Russian Government deemed it advisable to do was to propose the formation at Orenburg of a philanthropic society with the object of rescuing Russian prisoners from bondage. Subscriptions were collected from private sources, and the Government granted to the society a secret subsidy of 3,000 roubles. Apart, however, from the question of means, the process of ransoming prisoners was a difficult one to carry out; and it was feared that the tribes of Central Asia might learn from what source the projected philanthropic society derived the greater part of its funds; in which case they would have concluded that the Russian Government feared the Khivans and in its dealings with them was obliged to use money payments instead of force.

The philanthropic society, then, was abandoned; and General Perofski, military governor of Orenburg, was requested to furnish the Minister of War with a detailed plan of campaign against Khiva, which was to be made in the disguise of a scientific expedition under military escort. Delay, however, was now caused by local reasons. There were disturbances among the Kirghiz tribes in the Orenburg district and in Siberia; and this occupied the whole attention of the local administration. In 1834, in order to strengthen the influence of Russia over the wandering tribes near the Caspian, and thus put an end to the existing state of insecurity, the fortress of Novo Alexandrovsk was constructed at the head of Kultuk bay; and to defend the rest of what then constituted the boundaries of the empire in this direction against the incursions of the Kirghizes, it was decided to erect a wall and ditch of 100 versts (67 miles) in length along the whole of that part of the boundary which was not protected by any natural bulwarks. This was the defence which was to have filled the gap in the Orenburg line, from the north of Tuguzaki to the river Ori. A small portion of the wall—not more than eighteen versts—which was to have formed a continuous rampart like the Great Wall of China, was finished in 1836. The height of the wall was six feet, the depth of the ditch the same. It was hoped that the whole work would be finished in six years; and $2\frac{1}{2}$ millions of roubles were assigned for its execution.

This Orenburg line marked fifty years ago the boundary of the Russian empire on the Central Asian side.

An expedition under Colonel Mansuroff, consisting of some five or six hundred Cossacks, was sent in 1836 against a Kirghiz tribe known to be in alliance with the Khivans, and which habitually aided them in their depredations. It was determined, however, that active measures must be taken against the Khivans themselves; and, all negotiations for the liberation of Russian prisoners at Khiva having failed, a measure was decided upon which had previously been taken into consideration and rejected.

In the year 1836 all the Khivan merchants who were returning to Orenburg and Astrakhan from the fair of Nijni Novgorod, were detained with their merchandise; and the Khan was informed that they would not be set free until the Russian captives in Khiva were liberated and all hostile action against the Russians brought to an end.

"It became evident," says the official historian of Perofski's expedition, "that any further delay or hesitation on the part of the Russians would be looked upon as timidity and would have the effect of increasing the audacity of the Khivans. It was therefore resolved to punish them by force of arms, and General Perofski received orders to advance with a large force on Khiva."

But during the high flooding of the river Amu the whole of the Khanate is liable to inundation, and as the chief floods take place there twice in the year—

the first in May and June, and the second in July and August—the time was considered most inconvenient for the advance of a military force towards Khiva.

Moreover, the greater part of the Khivans could easily, in case of a hostile invasion during the winter, collect their corn, cattle, slaves, and all their property, and seek shelter for a time in the neighbouring steppe, or else, in Perofski's words, " fly to another territory of Khiva, beyond the barren sands, and forming another oasis with its town of Merv." Consequently the force destined for the expedition to Khiva could not rely, in case it arrived there in winter, on finding any considerable stock of provisions; and it was therefore thought necessary to reach Khiva while the corn was yet standing in the fields.

"The Khivans," according to our Russian authority, "notwithstanding their rapacity, are not a warlike race; and although the Khan would be able, in case of war, to bring into the field a mounted force of 20,000 men, this force had no regular formation or discipline, was badly armed, and was, therefore, incapable of offering any serious resistance. The Khivan artillery consisted at that time of about a dozen unwieldy guns. Their powder was of bad quality, the cannon balls were of irregular forms, and as they did not fit the calibre of the guns, the Khivans wrapped them in felt and so rammed them down. The artillerymen were generally Russian prisoners, and they possessed but little skill."

Khiva, then, could afford but scanty means of support for an invading army; and it was necessary for the troops to take with them all the requisite supplies for the whole period of the campaign. Nor could they calculate on obtaining fresh horses and camels to replace those which would be lost on the route from exhaustion and other causes. Arrangements for transport had, therefore, to be made on a large scale, and measures adopted for forwarding to the Line, in case of need, not only provisions, but also camels and horses. These were the chief obstacles which had to be taken into account in drawing up the plan of the campaign; and it was necessary to keep in view the great difference between campaigning in the desert steppes and in populous Europe.

In European campaigns (putting Turkey aside) a scarcity of water is hardly ever experienced, and it is seldom necessary for the troops to supply themselves with water for the day's march. Troops advance along established roads, through cultivated and inhabited districts, in which not only quantities of provisions can be had for the army, but where there are very often means for furnishing the force with horses, clothing, and ammunition.

But in Central Asia a scarcity of water is one of the principal difficulties attending an expedition; constituting a great source of anxiety to the commander. There are no established roads, the soldiers are obliged to march by companies, or under the direction of a guide; the wandering natives retreat at the approach of strangers; and perhaps after marching a hundred versts not a soul is to be met with, nor any information to be obtained as to the position of the enemy. Local resources for supplying a force with provisions do not exist; everything must, consequently, follow in the train of the attacking forces. The boundless and exposed character of the steppes facilitate flank movements; attacks, therefore, must be expected from all sides, and the ordinary disposition of the force must be in square, or some such order.

A military expedition in Central Asia is, in fact, only a caravan or train, following no regular route, always suffering from want of water or fuel, and liable at each halt to have its horses and camels driven away, and consequently to be deprived of its means of advancing. The train of an expeditionary force in the steppe, where everything must follow the troops, is necessarily a large one. A European force of 1,000 men can be limited to twenty or thirty waggons, or one waggon to every 40 or 50 men; whereas, in the Khivan expedition of 1839, each soldier had to be provided with two camels, while to every two camels one Kirghiz was attached. Although the Kirghizes were absolutely indispensable to the force on account of their knowledge of the nature and habits of the camels, and of their acquaintance with the steppe, the Russians could not place full confidence in them; and, in case of a hostile attack, it would be necessary to take measures to prevent them not only from running away, but also from communicating with the hostile Kirghizes and Khivans, and assisting them to drive away the horses and camels of the Russians. Thus a military expeditionary force in the steppes is, in the words of the Russian historiographer, "only an escort for the protection of its own baggage and provision train."

In reference to two previous Russian marches to Khiva, that of the Yaitsk Cossacks in 1610, and of Prince Bekovitch in 1717, only scanty and incomplete accounts, founded on inquiries and conjectures, were in existence at the period of the expedition contemplated by Perofski. Captain Mouravieff, who was at Khiva in 1819, had written a description of the route thither from Krasnovodsk, that is, from the Caspian Sea; but being kept in confinement at Khiva, and in danger of losing his life, he could not collect and verify native accounts relating to Khiva and to the routes leading thither from the Orenburg-Uralsk cordon-line. The information given by travellers who had visited Khiva, and by fugitives from that country, was still less satisfactory. Some accounts carefully gathered from Russian prisoners released in 1837-39 related only to Khiva itself. Respecting the routes leading to Khiva, and with reference to the surrounding steppe, they could of course give no correct data.

Thus in 1839 the Russians were in possession of reliable information in regard only to the northern, that is to say, the most accessible and most explored part of the steppe. The southern portion and the routes leading from it to Khiva, over a distance of 700 versts, were only known by verbal accounts, which were inaccurate, obscure, and conflicting, having been obtained from uncultivated Russian prisoners from Khiva, or from Asiatics unworthy of full credit.

In addition to striking changes in the weather, the grass during winter is covered with a crust of ice; and as the horses, camels, and cattle are only fed on grass, the deep snow and ice deprive them of pasturage, and expose them to death from starvation.

It will be seen from the foregoing account that the principal difficulty in organising the expedition lay in provisioning the force, and in providing the requisite means for its transport. The length of the route, extending over 1,000 versts, about 500 of which passed through a barren steppe, rendered the conveyance of all the stores by the same camels impossible for the whole distance. It was, therefore, found necessary to form a dépôt of provisions, &c. at a point in the interior of the steppe, as near Khiva as possible, and to provide other means for transporting the stores to this point; whence the troops, being furnished with the requisite supplies of food, ammunition, &c., might push forward to Khiva on camels. That is to say, as a preliminary measure, it was necessary to select, on the route fixed upon for the march of the expeditionary force, a convenient point for the erection of a fortification and the formation of a dépôt, having in its vicinity an abundant supply of water and grass.

The plan of the campaign was drawn up on the following basis :—I. The principal detachment against Khiva to consist of 5,000 men, of which 3,000 would be sufficient for inflicting punishment on Khiva; the remainder of the force to be employed in guarding the dépôt of stores at the intermediate point. The force to consist of troops of the Orenburg corps. II. All preparations for the expedition to be made at Orenburg, on account of the greater convenience and economy of this arrangement, and the possibility of superintendence by the authorities; the main body of the force to march from Orenburg. III. A detachment to be sent in advance for selecting, on the route to Khiva, the most convenient spot for establishing a dépôt, and for fortifying within it the garrison entrusted with its keeping. IV. To transport the stores gradually, on carts furnished from Orenburg, to the point in the steppe chosen for the intermediate dépôt. V. In order to protect the transport train despatched from the frontier to the intermediate dépôt against hostile Kirghizes and Khivans, to form a separate detachment, independent of the main body of the force. VI. The transport of all provisions, &c., for the main body as well as for the troops themselves, from the dépôt to Khiva, to be performed by camels; for which purpose the requisite number of these animals to be obtained and collected during the summer from the Kirghiz tribes under Russian subjection. VII. After the occupation of Khiva, or any other town of the Khanate, all further military operations to be regulated by circumstances.

The conduct of the campaign was entrusted to General Perofski, at that time military governor of Orenburg.

CHAPTER III.

THE FIRST RUSSIAN AGENT IN AFGHANISTAN.

IN 1837, when General Perofski was already occupied with preparations for his expedition against Khiva, a military and political agent, Capt. Vitkievitch (called by Burnes, Kaye, and other English writers "Vickovitch"), was despatched by the Russian Government to Cabul, whence he was to proceed to Lahore; and both at Cabul and at Candahar he offered a Russian alliance, with subsidies and arms, in view of an attack upon Herat and upon Runjeet Singh's possessions in India.

According to a Russian official report dated Sept. 30 (Oct. 12), 1837, the intelligence received at Teheran of the arrival of Burnes at Cabul had induced Count Simonitch to send Vitkievitch thither; and this may be perfectly true. But before Burnes's arrival at Cabul, at the beginning of Sept., 1837,

Count Simonitch had written to Dost Mahomed expressing a wish to befriend him; and in forwarding to the Secretary of the Indian Government a copy of the Count's letter, Burnes pointed out that the Russian ambassador had " himself commenced the correspondence with the chief of Cabul, telling him that if the Shah of Persia would not assist him his court was ready to do so."

Dost Mahomed's agent at Teheran, in transmitting the ambassador's letter, had written as follows: " The Russian ambassador, who is always with the Shah, has sent you a letter which I enclose. The substance of his verbal message is that if the Shah does everything you want so much the better; and if not the Russian Government will furnish you with everything wanting. The object of the Russians is to have a road to the English (India); and for this they are very anxious."

It is to be observed that in the original mutilated and garbled version of the "*Correspondence Relating to Cabul and Afghanistan,*" the letter from which the above passages are cited had been omitted. It was published for the first time in 1859, when no one was thinking of Afghanistan or of Russia. The edition of 1859, with the restored passages printed between brackets, recalls the words of Prince Bismarck, who, asked in the Chamber why Prussia, unlike the other European Governments, published no collections of diplomatic documents, replied that to prepare such documents for the use of the public it would be necessary to "double the number of clerks employed in the Foreign Office."

The Ameer had, on his side, written to the Emperor of Russia complaining that the English were supporting Shah Shoojah; that they were on good terms with Runjeet Singh; that they did not seem favourably disposed towards him, Dost Mahomed; that the Sikhs were his enemies; and that he hoped the Emperor would "arrange matters in the Afghan country" and allow the Ameer "to be received, like the Persians, under the government of Russia."

The letter from the Emperor Nicholas in reply, though it contained no direct promise of assistance, was thought sufficiently compromising by the English Foreign Office to be suppressed. So also was a passage in a letter from Count Simonitch referring to the fact that Vitkievitch had gone to Cabul as bearer of an autograph letter from the Czar, and another passage setting forth that the presents he was charged to offer came from "the Imperial store."

The presents offered by Burnes had been, in accordance with his formal instructions on the subject, " of moderate value ; " and he felt it necessary to apologise for their poorness, and to explain that they had no governmental character, but were his own personal gifts. General Hanlan, an American officer who commanded Dost Mahomed's regular troops, and acted as Chief of the Staff to the entire army, has told us in his volume on Afghanistan that Burnes's offerings were despised, and that they were regarded with contempt even by the ladies of the harem among whom they were distributed.

The arrival of Vitkievitch at Cabul, bearing rich presents, was to the Ameer something more than annoying ; and though he could neither accept the support of England, involving as it did his abandonment of Peshawur, nor that of Russia, which was conditional on his recognising the claims of Persia over Herat, the interference of Russia in his affairs had, all the same, the effect of bringing about a war between England and Afghanistan.

The Russians were quite satisfied with the result attained ; for the official historian of Perofski's expedition writes that the Russian agent "contrived to acquire the friendship of Dost Mahomed of Cabul, whom he succeeded in disposing favourably towards Russia."

Vitkievitch had received only verbal instructions, and, according to the Russian writer just cited, he was "not to disclose anywhere that he was sent by the Government." But Vitkievitch said everywhere who and what he was, and wore habitually the uniform of a Cossack officer. This strange demeanour on the part of a Russian agent caused a certain amount of mystification. Vitkievitch was described as a " Russian from Moscow," an " Anatolian," a " Cossack ; " and one of the English agents, on being informed that he was a Pole, pronounced this statement not only untrue but "disgusting;" since no one, he said, could conceive a Pole entering the service of Russia.

Vitkievitch, however, was really a Pole; and he had not been consulted as to whether or not he would enter the Russian service. Convicted in 1824, when a student at Wilna, of having organized a secret society called the Black Brothers, and of having written " revolutionary letters and verses," he was transported to Orenburg, and drafted as private into one of the battalions of the Orenburg corps. Six years afterwards he was, on the recommendation of his colonel, and in consideration of his praiseworthy conduct, talents, and knowledge of the Persian and Kirghiz language, promoted to the grade of under-officer, and attached to the Orenburg Boundary Commission. In 1831 he performed brilliant military service in the Kirghiz country, and his reports were declared in an official document to be "full of interesting information and remarks, so that not one of his predecessors in the steppe has been able to form so correct a judgment of the Kirghiz tribes or of their relations to each other." In August of the same year the chief of the Orenburg corps recommended Vitkievitch for a commission, observing that, with the exception of a certain "secretiveness of disposition, the natural result of so many misfortunes," his behaviour was all that could be desired. Vitkievitch, however, in spite of his services and of the good opinion with which he had inspired his superior officers, did not receive his commission until 1834, when he is said to have owed it in some measure to the representations of the illustrious Humbolt, whose acquaintance he had made at St. Petersburg, and who interested himself greatly on Vitkievitch's behalf. After his expedition to Bokhara he was advanced one step, and on his return to St. Petersburg from Cabul, at the end of April, 1839, he was recommended for promotion in the Guards, besides being decorated and having a sum of money allotted to him.

At Cabul, whether from a wish to inspire confidence in return, or with the direct object of alarming the English, Vitkievitch gave freely the sort of news that one would have expected him to withhold. Thus he told Burnes that General Barofski was commanding the forces before Herat and that the Russians were about to send against Khiva that expedition under General Perofski (with whom General Barofski was naturally confounded in the journals of the period) which the English believed to have arrived in Khiva long before it had started from Orenburg. The Russians indeed waited to make their attack on Khiva "until the settlement of English matters in Afghanistan; in order that the influence and impression of the Russian proceedings in Central Asia might have more weight, and that England, in consequence of her own conquests, might no longer have any right to trouble the Russian Government for explanations."

Vitkievitch was a friend of Count Soltykoff, well-known by his travels in Persia and in India; and he had repeatedly shown the Count a pistol with which he intended, he said, some day or other to shoot himself. Soon after his return to St. Petersburg from the mission to Cabul, Vitkievitch in fact, blew his brains out; leaving behind him a letter from which it appeared that he suffered from no one grievance in particular, but was discontented with the world in general. A disturbance had recently taken place at Wilna in which he feared that his brother might have been implicated. But this affords no direct clue to his suicide, since he afterwards ascertained that his brother was not concerned in the outbreak. The night before his suicide he was at the theatre with Prince Soltykoff, apparently in excellent spirits; and before retiring to bed he gave orders to be called early the next morning. He seems to have killed himself with deliberation; and before doing so, he destroyed all the papers, including copies of his correspondence with the English agents in Afghanistan, which he was to have embodied in a report for the Asiatic department of the Russian Foreign Office.

Of the arguments and promises employed by

Vitkievitch in his dealings with the chiefs of Candahar and with the Ameer of Cabul, we have sufficient knowledge from the reports transmitted by Burnes to the Indian Government. The Russian agent, as Lieut. Leech sent word from Candahar to Burnes at Cabul, was offering money for a war against the Sikhs, with a view to the reconquest of Mooltan and Derajat and for regaining Scinde. The Russians would send arms, moreover, but not men; and the Sirdars of Candahar were informed that " the English had preceded the Russians in civilization for some generations, but that now the latter had arisen from their sleep and were seeking for foreign possessions and alliances ; and that the English were not a military nation, but merely the merchants of Europe."

At Cabul, Vitkievitch informed the Ameer that " the Emperor of Russia was supreme in his dominions and could act of himself with promptitude and without being delayed by having to consult others while the British Government transacted its business by a Council which gave rise to procrastination. This would show him the advantage of allying himself to Russia, where no such inconvenience existed." After quitting Cabul, some weeks later than

Burnes, Vitkievitch wrote the Ameer a letter upbraiding him with his hesitancy, and reproaching him, for not having had the sense to accept either the English or the Russian alliance. Thus, whatever his Government may have thought, Vitkievitch himself would seem to have been dissatisfied with the result of his mission. His early adventure in the character of Polish patriot, the enterprise he displayed in the steppes and on his journey to Bokhara, his arrival and virtual proclamation, both at Bokhara and at Cabul, of the business on which he was engaged, together with his energy and activity as a soldier, a student and an observer, prove him to have been a man of high spirit; and he may have regarded his mission to the Ameer as a failure. One effect which in any case it produced was to raise apprehensions on the part of Afghanistan, with consequences sufficiently well-known.

While Vitkievitch was pursuing his intrigues at Cabul and Perofski was preparing for his expedition to Khiva, Herat was being besieged by a Persian force strengthened by a regiment of so-called Russian deserters, under the leadership of General Samson himself a Russian; the siege operations being under the general direction of the before-mentioned General Barofski. Count Simonitch, too, Russian Ambassador at Teheran, took an active part in the siege, and distributed large sums of money among the Persian troops, to whom arrears of pay were due.

Thanks to the energy of a young English officer, Lieut. Pottinger, of the Bombay Artillery, the defence was prolonged for a period of nine months. Meanwhile England had made diplomatic representations at Teheran, and what was probably more effective had sent an expedition to the Persian Gulf; and according to the Shah of Persia, who made a public declaration on the subject, it was owing to pressure from England that in Sept., 1838, the siege was raised.

CHAPTER IV.

PEROFSKI'S EXPEDITION.

"FROM the times of John the Terrible," says the official historian of Perofski's expedition, "the Russians have always sought means for opening a channel for their trade through Central Asia with India, in order to acquire some of that fabulous wealth for which India was always so famous; but it was Peter the Great who was first enabled to take energetic measures in this direction."

The successors of Peter the Great, following out his views, cherished the idea of establishing themselves in Central Asia, and thus opening a new route for Russian commerce to the East. We have seen that in furtherance of these views, Aboul-Hair-Khan, Sultan of the Lesser Horde, with the Kaisaks under his rule, was received, in 1730, under the protection of Russia, and a commencement was then made towards the subjugation of the Kirghiz steppes, which also led to the establishment of intercourse with the neighbouring Khanates of Khiva and Bokhara.

At this period the Russian Government had, in the words of the official historian, " become acquainted with the extreme difficulty of penetrating into Central Asia and further into India." It therefore turned its attention exclusively to the organization of the south-eastern boundaries of the empire, which, for a long time, during the whole of the eighteenth century were the scenes of disturbances between the various tribes established there. Thus, first the disorders in the Kirghiz steppes, the insurrections of the Bashkirs, and the flight of the Kalmucks into Chinese territories; and, lastly, in 1773 and 1774, the Pugacheff, rebellion, absorbed the attention of the Government, and diverted its views from all projects in the east.

It has been mentioned in a previous chapter that in 1793, at the request of the Khan, the Empress Catherine II. sent her oculist Blankenagel to Khiva. The Khan determined to keep him under surveillance as long as any necessity for his medical skill existed; after which he was to be sent back to Russia, but before arriving at his destination was to be murdered, in order that he should not relate anything he had seen. Blankenagel hearing of this sought safety in flight, and he contrived to gain over several Turcomans, who got him safely to Mangishlak, whence he made his way by sea to Astrakhan.

In 1819 a mission was sent to Khiva, under the command of Captain Mouravief. But this Embassy was also received with distrust, and we have seen that it led to nothing.

The Russian Government, recognizing the advantages of the trade with Bokhara, and seeing that this trade was rendered very precarious by the rapacity of the Kirghizes and Khivans, and that the passage of caravans was attended every year with great danger, despatched an Embassy to Bokhara in 1819 (simultaneously with the mission of Mouravief to Khiva) in order to concert measures with the Khan of Bokhara for ensuring and strengthening commercial relations; but the Emir, or Khan, of Bokhara, though promising a friendly reception for the caravans, would not undertake to protect their passage through the Kirghiz steppes, but left that duty entirely to Russian escorts. It was consequently considered most advantageous to establish a trading company, which should enjoy the exclusive right of trade with Central Asia; the company was to have a working capital of 6,000,000 roubles, and to possess its own camels, so as to avoid any obstacles and delays in the transport of goods. To convey the caravans of the company, it was proposed to give an escort of 280 men, with two guns, who were to be maintained at the cost of the company, and who were also to be allowed to erect a caravan-sarai and fortifications on the Syr-Daria and on the points of the caravan route. But as it was impossible to create such a company in a short time, and as it was uncertain whether it could ever be formed by Russian merchants, it was proposed in the meantime to furnish the ordinary caravans with an escort at the expense of the Government, and to charge the outlay under this head to the Custom House dues of the Orenburg region. A caravan was accordingly despatched to Bokhara in 1824, under the protection of 500 men; it was, however, encountered by the Khivans, who plundered part of it. The other part returned. On this occasion the loss suffered by private individuals amounted to 547,000 roubles; while the expense to the Government in furnishing the convoy was 224,000 roubles. Thus the attempt failed, and naturally in such a state of affairs the company could not be formed.

In addition to crippling Russian trade in the East by the constant plunder of caravans and inciting the Kirghizes to commit these depredations, the Government of Khiva had long encouraged the pirates of the Caspian, who kidnapped Russian fishermen on that sea in great numbers every year, and sold them in all the markets of the East, and particularly in Khiva. These unfortunate prisoners were doomed to pass their lives in hard toil, suffering every privation; and they usually ended their insupportable lives under the blows of their task-masters, whose Mahommedan creed freed them from all considerations of humanity with respect to "Kafirs" or unbelievers, while the civil law gave them irresponsible power over the lives of their slaves.

Already in the eighteenth century the Russian Government had tried to devise means for the liberation of Russian prisoners in the East. Thus by an ukaz of the 28th January, 1767, hostages were ordered to be seized for the purpose of compelling the Asiatics to exchange them for Russian prisoners. This measure was quite justifiable; seeing, as the official writer puts it, that "the

Khivans and Bokharians traded and lived in safety along the Orenburg and Siberian lines and at Astrakhan, while Russian merchants could not enter Central Asiatic territory without running a risk of falling into life-long bondage. The distance and inaccessibility of the Khanates of Central Asia proved, and still prove, a serious obstacle to adopting more effectual measures for the liberation of prisoners."

The attempts of the Russian Government to obtain the release of prisoners by negotiation were not attended with success, and everything showed that it was quite useless to treat with the Governments of Khiva and Bokhara. Correspondence and negotiations led to nothing. The best proof of this is said to have been afforded by Negri's mission to Bokhara in 1820, and that of Demaison in 1833, which did not mend matters in the least. The Bokharians from that time forward always tried to evade the question of Russian prisoners, never thought of surrendering them, and continued purchasing them in spite of their formal agreement with M. Negri, and in defiance of all the rights of humanity. And if this was the practice of the Emir of Bokhara, who had striven to maintain friendly relations with Russia, the Khan of Khiva who had always been at enmity with Russia, did not, even for the sake of appearances, attempt to disguise his dealings. His territories were equally inaccessible to all Christians.

The Government at last assigned 3,000 roubles for the redemption of Russian prisoners. This, however, likewise led to nothing. The slave-holders refused to accept any ransom, as they found it more profitable to retain their hard-working bondsmen. There was extreme difficulty, moreover, in liberating the prisoners by other means than through intermediate agents, who, if caught, were liable to be put to death or made slaves. In 1830 the position of the question of Russian prisoners in Central Asia was, according to authentic accounts as follows :—

" Incited by the high prices obtained by Russian prisoners, the Kirghizes kidnapped them even on the Line, and disposed of them in the neighbouring countries of Central Asia, principally at Khiva, where, according to reliable information received at the time, there were more than 2,000 Russians in bondage. In remote times men were seized from settlements in the interior, even on the Volga and beyond that river, and subsequently on the Line. But about the year 1830, Russian fishermen on the Caspian used alone to be kidnapped by Kirghizes and Turcomans at the rate of 200 every year. Russian prisoners were sold at Khiva, in the bazaars, and this traffic was participated in not only by the highest Khivan officials, but also by Khivan traders who visited Russia, and who, when frequenting the Kirghiz encampments for the purposes of trade, incited the Kirghizes to make prisoners, buying them up beforehand, and giving money in advance. Although the Orenburg Frontier Commission had at its disposal the sum of 3,000 roubles for the redemption of Russian prisoners, it was able only to procure the liberation of a very small number, as sentence of death was awarded at Khiva to anyone who consented to sell his slave in order that he might be restored to his native country."

The Russian prisoners, while sinking under hard labour and suffering under privations of every description, were carefully guarded; and for a first attempt to escape they were deprived of their nose and ears, a second attempt being punished by torture and death. Very few, therefore, ventured to fly, knowing the severe punishment that awaited

G

them in case they were retaken. To deter slaves as much as possible from attempting to escape, many were forced to marry native women, and different expedients were employed to convert them to the Mahommedan faith. In order to diminish this system of man-stealing, efforts were made to detain Kirghizes belonging to the same tribe as the kidnappers. But even this failed; and it was felt to be unjust to make a whole tribe answerable for the delinquencies of some of its members. The prisoners, meanwhile, took advantage of every opportunity to implore succour; and their helpless families assailed the local authorities with their prayers, and even accused them of intentionally allowing their relatives to remain in captivity.

Under such circumstances it was "necessary to have recourse to decided and final measures." These were to "lay an embargo on all the persons and property of the subjects of Khiva in Russian territory until the liberation of Russian prisoners, and if this should not have the desired effect to compel restitution by force of arms," the adoption of this latter alternative being repeatedly urged on the Government by the local Russian authorities. The events of 1830 to 1832, and especially the Polish insurrection diverted all the attention of the Government towards the west. But a few years later Russia determined to adopt strong measures against Khiva, and the recommendations of a Special Committee, approved by his Imperial Majesty on the 24th March, 1839, were as follows:—

1st. To commence at once the organisation of an expedition against Khiva, and to establish the necessary dépôts and stations on the route without delay.

2nd. To conceal the real object of the expedition, which was to be given out as a scientific expedition to the Aral sea.

3rd. To postpone the departure of the expedition until the settlement of English matters in Afghanistan, in order that the influence and impression of the Russian proceedings in Central Asia might have more weight, and that England, in consequence of her own conquests, might no longer have any right to trouble the Russian Government for explanations; on no account, however, to delay the expedition later than the spring of 1840.

4th. In the event of the expedition terminating successfully, to replace the Khan of Khiva by a trustworthy Kaisak Sultan, to establish order and security as far as possible, and to give full freedom to the Russian trade.

5th. To assign 425,000 silver roubles and 12,000 gold ducats, for the estimated cost of the expedition, and to supply the detachment with arms and the indispensable material, and to allow the Governor-General of Orenburg to avail himself of the assistance of the local artillery and engineer force.

Soon after (on the 10th October, 1839), final dispositions were issued for the Russian operations after the occupation of Khiva; and a formal instrument was drawn up for the guidance of the future Khan of Khiva, defining his relations towards Russia, and guaranteeing peace between the two countries.

Thus at the outside of the limit of the time proposed for the expedition, that is from the spring of 1839 to the spring of 1840, there remained only a year for making the necessary preparations. Circumstances, however, compelled the departure of the expedition eight months earlier than had been originally contemplated. The reasons for hastening the expedition were, " First, the important consideration that if the detachment were to leave Orenburg early in the spring of 1840, it would have to traverse the arid saline steppes, while on the other hand the lateness of the autumn and winter of 1839 were considered particularly favourable for the march of the troops, inasmuch as a sufficient supply of cold water could be obtained on the route; and, secondly, the efforts of the English at this period to penetrate into Central Asia with the object of establishing their influence there and inciting the Khivans to offer an obstinate resistance to Russia.

"No one," continues the official historian, "can seriously affirm that the English are not anxious for the welfare of these nations; but all, we trust, will agree with us when we say that, nevertheless, the interests of England are held by them paramount to everything. It is also generally known that the English have from remote times diligently watched the progress of events in the whole world (in the interests of Great Britain, be it observed), and that they are always troubled and dissatisfied if fate allows any other nation to have influence over the progress of mankind. This is the policy of the ancient Phœnicians and Carthaginians, and of the modern Venetians, Genoese, Spaniards, and Dutch—in one word, this is the policy of maritime and commercial powers."

It is not astonishing, therefore, that the English, not being thoroughly acquainted with the existing state of affairs in Central Asia, should have been considerably alarmed at the Russian proceedings in the Kirghiz steppe; nor that they should have attributed the measures adopted by the Russian Government for securing the boundaries and trade of the empire to aggressive projects, and even to the old project of penetrating into India. Hence arose a natural desire on the part of the English to ascertain the real importance, in a political respect, of the possession of the Central Asiatic steppes by Russia, and the probability of her penetrating thence into Indian territory.

From 1824, therefore, a succession of English agents, regardless of all obstacles, penetrated into Central Asia, and some of them even returned to their native country through Russia. At first, in the year 1830, many Englishmen, " under motives entirely evangelical," says the Russian historian, settled in the town of Orenburg. "But when it was perceived that these missionaries turned their attention to other matters, they were requested to leave. Losing all hope of extending their interest in Central Asia from the side of Russia, the English commenced penetrating thither principally from India and through Persia. Thus from 1824 Central Asia was visited by Moorcroft, Conolly, Wolf, Burnes, and Strange, and later by Stoddart, Abbott, Shakespear, and again by Burnes near the time of the Russian Khiva expedition, or during the very period."

All the persons here enumerated, with the exception of Wolf—the brave missionary who travelled to Bokhara without escort or protection of any kind to save the Jewish inhabitants from the terrible persecution to which they had lately been subjected —were in the service of the East India Company; and of course it was not, in the words of the official historian, " curiosity alone and their own affairs that allured them into Central Asia." While these English agents were collecting every possible information on the spot, the Russians had no means of following their example, and were even unacquainted with their movements. The visits of the English agents to the various Khanates, and the details of their journeys, became only known to Russia incidentally through their published works; which, of course, did not contain all the results of their investigations. All the direct information that the Russians could procure was meagre and obscure, and was supplied to them by Asiatics, who, either through ignorance or timidity, were not always able to furnish important and trustworthy accounts. Owing to a want of officials well acquainted with the Oriental languages, it was found necessary to confide in uneducated Asiatics, or to employ agents who, being ignorant of the Oriental languages, were obliged to have interpreters attached to them. "The principal purveyors of intelligence to the Russians were consequently almost always Mahommedans, who, being involuntarily under the influence of the rulers of Central Asia, in whom, under the *régime* of Mahommedanism, was also centred the highest ecclesiastical power, did not discharge their duties very willingly, nor in a reliable manner; they were not always able to disclose all they knew, and were altogether very uncertain media of communication, notwithstanding that, as Mahommedans, they had in every respect much greater facilities than Christians for gaining access to the different countries of Central Asia."

As early as 1828 Alexander Burnes had commenced his survey of the Indus river; and having become convinced in 1830 of the navigability of the Indus over its whole course of about 700 miles, he represented to the English Government all the importance of this stream, both in political and commercial respects. At the same time some Russian goods which had by accident found their way to the banks of the Indus, led him to the conclusion that the rivalry between British and English manufacturers had already commenced at this point, and ¦he not only succeeded in convincing his Government as to this, but also induced it to believe in the possibility of the appearance of Russian political agents on the river Indus, and even of a Russian force.

" Here, then," says the official writer, " we have an explanation of the repeated attempts made by English agents to penetrate from India through the whole of Central Asia as far as the Russian boundaries, in order to assure themselves of the justness or otherwise of their apprehensions; and these movements on the part of the English were at the same time a source of serious alarm to the Russian Government."

The Russians had reliable information that the agents of the East India Company were continually appearing either at Khiva or Bokhara; they also believed that this enterprising Company, having enormous means at its command, was endeavouring not only to establish its influence throughout the whole of Asia, but was also desirous of extending the limits of its Asiatic possessions. The power of England, the industry and wealth of its people, the tendency of the English to act together in commercial associations, and lastly the cupidity of the Asiatic rulers — all these gave to the English great facilities for strengthening their influence in Central Asia, and for doing Russia "serious damage" by establishing regular commercial relations with Central Asia. It was only necessary to allow the possibility of the English supplying the Khivans and Turcomans, the nearest and most hostile neighbours of Russia, and likewise the Kirghizes, with arms and ammunition, in order to become convinced of the necessity of counteracting the schemes of England, "whose agents did not even try to conceal their hopes, in their published accounts, of becoming masters, not only of the whole trade between the river Indus and the Hindoo Kush, but likewise of the market of Bokhara, the most important in Central Asia."

It was accordingly decided in 1835, in order to watch the English agents and counteract their efforts, to send Russian agents into Central Asia, also to establish a Russian company, so as to enable Russia to compete with the English in trade. But although a small trading company was formed after the Khivan expedition, when the steppes had been rendered comparatively safe, even this company soon suspended operations. Meanwhile, in order to watch the march of events in Central Asia, the before-mentioned Captain Vitkevitch was despatched thither in the capacity of agent. In the winter of 1835 he had accidentally got to Bokhara, accompanied by some Kirghizes; and without concealing the fact of his being a Russian officer, he spent several months at Bokhara, and returned safely to Orenburg, proving his aptitude for such missions. "This officer," we are told "travelled several years in Persia and Cabul during the most interesting period of the English expedition to Afghanistan, contrived to acquire the friendship of Dost Mahomed of Cabul, whom he succeeded in disposing favourably towards Russia; and returned to St. Petersburg in 1839. Unfortunately, in the same year he committed suicide, destroying, before his death, all the materials he had collected."

Meanwhile the intelligence which reached the Russians from Central Asia in 1839 gave rise to further apprehensions. Tulia-Bergan, a caravan leader, on his return from Bokhara in the same year reported, " that twenty-five English had arrived at Khiva from Cabul with offers to the Khan of troops and money against the Russians." The reports of the appearance of English agents, and of their persistent interference in the relations between Khiva and Russia received confirmation at later periods; and as, at this time, the English forces had penetrated into Cabul, whence they had expelled Dost Mahomed, who was favourable to Russia, and were only divided from the territory of Bokhara by the Hindoo Kush, it was to these circumstances that the vacillation of the Khan of Khiva in the matter of the surrender of the Russian prisoners was attributed at Orenburg. It was, therefore, of the greatest importance to hasten the expedition for the punishment of Khiva, "so as to prevent the English from supporting the resistance of this Khanate against Russia, and to anticipate the possibility of any other Central Asiatic rulers being induced to join Khiva by means of any threats and promises of reward that might be employed by the English agents."

The English agents who were in Central Asia

during the years 1839 and 1840 were Abbott and Shakespear. In May, 1840, Captain Abbott, of the East India Company's service, reached Novo-Alexandrofsk fortress from Khiva, and proceeded thence to Orenburg. "Whether," says the Russian historiographers "Abbott had the intention to return home through Russia, or whether, like Burnes, he selected this route for the purpose of making a survey of the Caspian, and of the Russian fortresses on it, is subject to much doubt. In his communications, however, he styled himself English Chargé d'Affaires to the Russian Court. By the order of the Khan he was robbed and wounded, on his route to the Caspian, by a gang of Turcomans (who had even been instructed by their chiefs to kill him), and from Orenburg he was sent in a suitable manner to St. Petersburg, whilst the Afghans that had accompanied him were sent back to their native country." Shakespear, the other English officer, reached Orenburg viâ Novo-Alexandrofsk with the Russian prisoners who had been released from Khiva; he was likewise immediately sent on to St. Petersburg. Both these agents wished to take an active part in the Russian negotiations with Khiva, especially Shakespear, who desired to take credit for the release of the Russian prisoners. These, however, had "prior to his arrival at Khiva, been collected and registered by the Russian Cornet, Aitof." Shakespear, according to the Russian official historian, even quarrelled on the road with the Khivan envoy Ataniaz, in charge of the Russian prisoners, alleging that their delivery had been entrusted to him. During his stay at Orenburg he attempted to interfere in "local political matters," but was told that everything of a political nature was decided at St. Petersburg, whither he was despatched.

The objects of the expedition Perofski was about to undertake were, as set forth by the Russian official historian,—*(a)* To secure the south-eastern boundaries of the empire by the subjugation of the Kirghiz horde, which could not be effected without the punishment of Khiva, the chief author of all disturbances in the Kirghiz steppes ; *(b)* to secure the Russian trade with Central Asia by putting a stop to the plundering of caravans, which also could not be carried out without the punishment of Khiva ; *(c)* to release several thousands of Russians from cruel bondage ; *(d)* to establish, not the dominion, but the strong influence of Russia on the neighbouring Khanates for the reciprocal advantages of trade, and to prevent the influence of the East India Company, so dangerous to Russia, from taking root in Central Asia; and lastly *(e)* to take advantage of this favourable opportunity for the scientific exploration of Central Asia, by making a survey of the shores of the sea of Aral, and of the mouth of the river Amu, and settling the long-disputed question of the original course of this river to the Caspian.

The force with which General Perofski had been ordered to Khiva was to be taken from the Orenburg corps, which had never been in action, had never seen service of any kind in the field, and had never even assembled in camp. It was, in short, according to the official historian of the Perofski expedition (possibly General Perofski himself), altogether insufficient for military purposes. To improve the condition of the troops, General Perofski transferred all the battalions to new quarters and assembled them periodically in camps. "Although," says the official historian, "this could not make the infantry more martial, yet it had the effect of improving its discipline and drill."

The very composition of the Orenburg corps was likely to tell against it in a military point of view.

The seven battalions numbered, in April 1839, 8,999 men, of whom 4,403 were recruits; while of these recruits 2,527 were Polish exiles, and 1,694 either exiles or criminals.

The force ultimately despatched against Khiva consisted of 5,325 men with twenty-two guns and four rocket-stands. It carried with it mining tools, canvas pontoons, and two portable boats.

In the way of provisions, biscuits, buck-wheat, meat, salt, and corn-brandy (vodka) were carried; and in addition to this, cabbage, cucumbers, cheese, sheeps' fat, lard, onions, pepper, vinegar, and money.

Former experience in the steppe had proved that horses soon became worn out when fed on grass alone. It was therefore necessary, on the long march to Khiva, to carry a supply of forage; 15,828 poods of oats for the horses and 3,793 poods of flour, and 1,925 poods of salt for the camels were accordingly ordered to be provided; 10,000 poods of hay were obtained from the cordon posts, and hydraulically compressed for greater portability into bundles of 6 or 7 poods each, which were to be carried along with the force. Along the route to Khiva 20,000 poods of hay were stored at Bish

Tamok, 25,000 on the river Emba and at Aby-Yaksh, and 25,000 near Ak-Bulak.

Owing to the absence of any roads in the southern steppe, and because it was anticipated that the force would be obliged to march through heavy snows, it was deemed advisable to provide a larger quantity of spades, pick-axes, &c. The portable flat-bottomed boats, which were to be transported in separate parts, were to be employed for navigation on the Oxus, and for surveying the shores of the sea of Aral; each boat was armed with a swivel gun or falconet. Eighty arabas were prepared for transporting the sick, and each battalion was provided with the regulated quantity of hospital stores and drugs. In addition to these stores a large quantity of articles in Asiatic taste were bought at Nijni Novgorod for distribution as presents to the Kirghizes and Turcomans.

The principal difficulties that the expedition to Khiva was expected to encounter would be in the waterless steppes that surrounded the Khanate. It was known that there were wells along the Ust-Urt of a depth varying from fifteen to twenty and thirty fathoms. According to Kirghiz accounts, these wells were paved round with stone and protected from the drifting sand and straying cattle, by large stone slabs pierced with a small hole through which buckets could be lowered. A stone trough for watering cattle was generally attached to each well. Small caravans could consequently traverse these steppes with facility. But large caravans had been unable, in former years, to perform the journey through the Ust-Urt without dividing themselves into sections or échelons; because, in addition to the scarcity of water, the great depth of the wells presented serious obstacles, as, out of these, only ten or fifteen buckets of water could be raised in one hour, and consequently only 200 or 300 camels or horses watered in the course of twenty-four hours. The expeditionary force could not be divided up into small parties without great danger, and the various detachments would have been obliged to wait several days at the wells for water, while it was drawn up in ordinary buckets. A special portable water-lifting apparatus was devised, by means of which the water could be rapidly drawn from the wells and distributed through india-rubber conduits, either into the boats or into leather and canvas waterproof reservoirs fixed on wooden frames.

It was proposed to transport all the stores on

camels, with the exception of the pontoon boats, arabas, and sledges, which, on account of their weight, could not be carried by these animals. The falconets, however, were to be carried on the backs of camels, and so disposed as to be capable of being mounted and brought to bear on the enemy in a quarter of an hour. In order to spare the artillery horses as much fatigue as possible, the gun caissons that could not be carried on the backs of camels were yoked to camels, which were harnessed like oxen.

In order, also, to husband the strength of the infantry soldiers (so that in case of need they might be despatched like dragoons in flying detachments), it was resolved to transport a portion of the infantry on the spare camels, two men on each camel, changing the men by turns on the march.

Then this new difficulty presented itself—that of obtaining a great number of camels, the required quantity being provisionally estimated at 10,000.

As the stores and provisions were gradually purchased and prepared, it was necessary to transport them to Orenburg, and thence into the interior of the steppe to the intermediate dépôts. For this purpose 7,750 three-horse carts, with their drivers, were supplied by the Bashkirs, with the requisite number of officers and non-commissioned officers to superintend the operation.

On the 18th (30th) June the march of the expeditionary force was commenced by Colonel Heke being sent forward with a flying column, consisting of a platoon of infantry transported in carts, and 400 mounted Bashkirs with two howitzers, to Donguz-Tan; which had been selected as a convenient spot for a store dépôt. Colonel Heke described his advance in a series of letters addressed to General Perofski. In one of these he gives a droll account of the means he took for testing the martial character of the troops under his command. Having concealed himself behind Bakgir Hill, he awaited the arrival of the train of stores, which advanced to the hill in two divisions; when, as soon as the first échelon appeared in sight, he suddenly showed himself with his Bashkirs on the hill, "in order to cause an alarm among the train of followers, and to watch the result." It appears that the men conveying the stores took the Bashkirs for Khivans, and immediately despatched a messenger to the second division of the train with intelligence that a body of Khivan troops, to the number of 8,000, had been discovered on Bakgir Hill. In the meantime Captain Simbuigin formed square with the carts and waggons, and posting his guns at intervals on the sides of the square, awaited the attack of the supposed enemy. Very different was the effect produced by the reported appearance of the foe on the rear division of the train. A general panic ensued and it was with difficulty that the men were prevented from running away.

The rugged character of the country, intersected with gullies and in parts covered with deep sands and stagnant salines, added to the great heats which had set in, impeded the progress of the train of stores, which was only enabled to join Colonel Heke at Bakgir Hill by the 5th (17th) July. On the 17th (29th) July the train advanced a stage of seventeen versts to Aly mountain, on which journey fifty waggons had to be abandoned on the road in consequence of the horses breaking down with fatigue, and of the cart-wheels splitting from the heat. A halt was ordered to collect the carts left behind, to rest the horses, and to muster fresh strength for performing the tedious passage of forty versts which still remained to be done before reaching the dépôt point on the Ak-Bulak river. As for the whole distance of the intermediate stage to Chushka-Kul, no water or grass could be found, the Bashkirs supplied themselves with grass and water in leather bags. The march was resumed at 5 o'clock in the morning, and by 11 o'clock 17½ versts having been traversed, a halt was made. At 3 o'clock the march was resumed. The day was sultry, and there being no wind, stifling clouds of dust enveloped the column. The heat of the sun was as powerful as in the deserts of Africa, the thermometer showing from 32° to 38° Reaumur in the shade, and 42° to 45° Reaumur in the sun. After passing six versts the men began to suffer from thirst. All the water that still remained was mixed with vinegar and distributed among the troops, the officers considerately sharing their stock with the men. But even this was not sufficient. Men and horses fell down exhausted in numbers, and were only saved from death by being immediately bled. Messengers were despatched on the best horses to Chushka-Kul for water, and the detachment moving slowly forward discovered soon afterwards a small well at the side of the road with brackish water, and some muddy pools. These were soon drained dry. At length, about midnight, a portion of the train reached the

Chushka-Kul wells, and sent a supply of water to those who had been left behind. It was only on the 15th (27th) July that the whole caravan was gathered together on the banks of the Ak-Bulak, when the erection of the advanced Chushka-Kul fortification was at once commenced.

To save great expense it was determined to obtain camels by hire instead of purchase. Although the Kirghiz elders assembled at the first gathering received the intimation respecting the supply of camels with proper submission, nevertheless the demand, on account of its novelty, gave rise to many rumours. Hence at the second gathering, which was attended by the representatives of all the branches of the Bagulinsk, Kitinsk, and Churinoosk tribes, General Genz announced that what the Government expected from the Kaisaks was not idle discussion, but obedience to the wishes of the Emperor. He also informed them that in case they did not carry out the behests of His Majesty, these might possibly be executed without their consent and without any indemnification. To this all present unanimously replied that they were quite ready to fulfil the orders of the Government, and seven volunteered " to arrest and bring before the Sultan ruler all those evilly-disposed Kirghizes who, at the instigation of Khiva, purposed creating disturbances in the steppe by spreading false rumours respecting the Russian movements." A list of the quantity of camels to be supplied by each tribe was at once drawn up, and written instructions respecting their delivery were distributed to the different elders.

Some of the tribes, however, had not furnished their quota of camels by the time fixed, *i.e.*, the first of November; in consequence of which the expeditionary force started with only 9,500 camels, though about 900 more joined it on the first stages of the march. The whole number collected was 10,400. Camel-drivers were furnished by the Kirghizes, at the rate of one man to every four or five camels.

The unfavourable condition of the atmosphere, combined with the scarcity of fodder and the great prevalence of disease, occasioned considerable loss among the men and cattle belonging to the different trains. The mortality among the Bashkirs attached to the five trains amounted to 199 men, while the number of horses lost on the journey through disease and exhaustion was 8,869, or a third of the whole number employed. At the same time, the dampness of the turf-huts, the rapid change from the sultry heat of the day to the cold temperature at night, and the bad quality of the water at Ak-Bulak, had a pernicious effect on the health of the garrisons of the advanced fortified points, where, towards the end of October, the number of invalids amounted to 110, sick and infirm. The prevailing diseases were scurvy, nervous fever, dysentery, and ague.

With the approach of cold weather the sickness increased considerably; thus, by the middle of December there were 168 men under medical treatment at the Emba, and 164 at Ak-Bulak. The number of deaths at this period in the two forts from fevers, dysentery, dropsy, and chiefly scurvy, reached 93.

As soon as the greater portion of the stores for the expedition had been conveyed to the advanced dépôts by the first five trains, and the success of the arrangements made the possibility of commencing the campaign in October a matter of certainty, a store and provision train, or camel caravan, was despatched by way of experiment under Colonel Danilevski, who received instructions to direct his attention to everything relating to the caravan, such as the loading of the camels, the order to be observed in marching and halting, &c. This caravan, consisting of 1,128 camels, left Orenburg on the 21st October (1st November) under convoy of one company of infantry (234 men), one sotnia of Cossacks (116 men), and twenty-five artillerymen, with four light howitzers and sixteen camel-borne ammunition boxes, and proceeded to the Emba, where they were to await the main detachment. There was no snow then on the ground, but the progress of the caravan was considerably impeded by the slippery surface of the ground produced by the frost after a fall of rain. In spite of this the caravan reached the Emba by the 12th (24th) November, having travelled 500 versts, or one-third of the whole distance between Orenburg and Khiva, in twenty-three days.

CHAPTER V.

PEROFSKI'S EXPEDITION *(continued)*.

FROM the foregoing it was concluded that the journey to Khiva could be performed in sixty, or, at most, in sixty-five days but for the existence of a barren steppe which stretched ahead for 800 versts, necessitating the transport with the expedition of large supplies of fodder for the camels and horses which formed nearly half the train. While the stores were in course of conveyance from Orenburg into the interior of the steppe, experiments were tried with the galvanic battery and rockets; the pioneers were exercised in the construction of pontoon bridges; special boats to carry six pieces were built under the superintendence of Captain Bodisko; Kirghizes and camels were concentrated in the steppe; the regimental bands practised new marching airs in the public square at Orenburg; while companies of soldier-choristers mastered the difficulties of a martial song composed purposely for the expedition.

All the preparations for the campaign were made under the pretence of a scientific expedition to the sea of Aral; but the large quantity of stores that was being collected, the unusual activity displayed, the preparation of winter clothing for the troops, and the concentration of an extraordinarily large body of soldiers and camels, roused general suspicion at Orenburg respecting the professed objects of the expedition, and gave rise to all manner of rumours and surmises. As the preparations approached maturity the curiosity of the uninitiated public became more acute. The secret, however, was soon disclosed. The troops destined for the expedition were mustered in the town square a few days before their departure, and the following address from the commander of the Orenburg corps was read :—

"By order of His Majesty the Emperor, I am going to march with a portion of the troops under my command against Khiva. Khiva has for many years tried the long-suffering patience of a strong and magnanimous Power, and has at length brought down upon herself the wrath which her hostile conduct has provoked.

" Honour and glory to those who, by God's mercy, have been called upon to march to the rescue of their brethren languishing in slavery.

" Comrades! frost and snow-storms await us, and all the inevitable and harassing difficulties of a distant march in the steppe during winter. But all the necessary preparations have been carefully made, and your requirements anticipated as far as possible; your zeal, ardour, and bravery will ensure success, and victory. The troops of the Orenburg corps are, for the first time, marching in great force against the enemy. Russia is determined to punish Khiva, our insolent and faithless neighbour. In two months, with God's help, we shall be in Khiva; and there, for the first time in the capital of the Khanate, will the Russians, before the Cross and Bible, offer up fervent prayers for their Czar and country.

" I now address those troops who will remain to guard and protect the Orenburg frontier and their own homesteads. Fortune has not decreed that you should share with us the dangers and difficulties of the approaching campaign; but you, nevertheless, deserve the grace and favour of the Emperor. Men of every grade, both high and low, after taking leave of your comrades, who will march forth to seek the enemy, you will sacredly bear in mind your duty and your oath, and cheerfully do service for yourselves and your absent comrades, to whom you will accord a joyful and hearty welcome on their return from the distant and difficult journey they are now about to undertake."

After this address had been read, and divine service performed, the troops defiled past their commander, and were then formed into columns.

All the heavy stores which could not be despatched in the Bashkir trains, and with the caravans, were transported beyond the river Ural, and equally distributed among the columns.

The detachment, for greater facility of movement, provisionment, and pasturage, was divided into four columns in the following manner :—

The first column was formed of two companies of the 2nd Battalion of the Line, one sotnia of Ural Cossacks, two small howitzers, and 360 Kirghiz camel-drivers with 1,800 loaded camels.

The commander of the column was Lieutenant-General Tolmachef, who was, at the same time, in command of all the infantry of the detachment.

The second column consisted of two companies of No. 5 Battalion, fifty Bashkirs, fifty Orenburg Cossacks, two mountain howitzers, and 400 Kirghizes as drivers to 2,000 camels carrying heavy stores; Lieutenant-Colonel Kurminski, chief of all the artillery, was at the head of this detachment.

The third column comprised the 4th Battalion, a division of the Orenburg regiment of Cossacks, a sotnia of Ural Cossacks, two 12-pounder guns, two 6-pounders, and six small mortars ; rocket, mortar, artillery, boat, and pontoon attendants and trains ; camp hospital, the Staff of the detachment, and 600 Kirghizes, with 3,000 camels. This column was entrusted to Colonel Mansurof, a cavalry officer.

The fourth column consisted of two companies of No. 5 Battalion, one sotnia of Bashkirs, two howitzers, and 300 Kirghizes with 1,800 camels and stores, and was under the charge of Major-General Tsiolkovski, at that time also in command of all the Bashkir and Mescheriak forces.

Besides these four columns, two regiments of Ural Cossacks, with 1,800 camels, marched on the 19th November from the Lower Orenburg Line, under the command of Colonel Bizianoff, to join the main detachment. This contingent also entered into the constitution of the main force of the expedition; but in order to save unnecessary marches, it was despatched from the Kalmykovski fortress direct to the River Emba.

The first and second columns left Orenburg on the 14th (26th) and 15th (27th) November, by the Berdiano-Kuralinsk Line; and the third and fourth marched on the 16th and 17th November in the direction of the Iletskaya Zachita. All these columns were to unite near Caravan Lake in the right bank of the Ilek river (a left affluent of the Ural river), and about seventeen versts from Grigorievsk Post on the Line. Here, before crossing the frontier, an order of the day was read to the troops, informing them that His Imperial Majesty the Emperor had been graciously pleased to invest General Perofski with the powers and privileges of a commander of a separate corps in the field.

Before the commencement of the march the whole detachment was so organized as to meet the special exigences of a winter and steppe campaign; separate instructions were issued for the discharge of camp and other military duties during the expedition; and a system of signalling between the different columns was adopted.

The columns, as independent parts of the whole detachment, were formed of infantry, cavalry, and artillery, with a proportionate number of load-camels.

Two hours before sunrise a general *réveillé* was sounded. The men then got up, breakfasted, took down their tents, and packed their luggage. At about 5 or 6 o'clock men were mustered for loading the camels; the convoying Cossacks proceeded to their posts, and made the Kirghizes lead the camels to the packs, while the other men of the column were told off in parties of six to load the camels. The order of loading, and the proper distribution of the stores on the backs of the camels, was superintended by officers. After the camels had been laden, the men proceeded to equip and arm themselves; some of them then mounted camels. When the Cossacks had mounted their horses, the advance guard started forward at a trot, the whole body following in several caravan lines. Camels loaded with the same description of stores followed each other in a line or a file.

Two Kirghizes were attached to every ten camels. One rode in front, and the other walked at the side, urging on the flagging animals and adjusting their loads. Whenever it was necessary to stop a camel for this latter purpose, it was taken out of the file, so as not to hinder the camels following behind, and afterwards placed at the end of its file. Or if left behind too great a distance, it would proceed with the rear-guard until the night halt.

Each file of camels was placed in charge of six Cossacks, who maintained order and assisted the camel-drivers. A Cossack rode in front of each file to show the way; these leading Cossacks endeavouring, as far as they could, to ride abreast.

The other troops marched with the advance and rear-guards and at the sides of the column. The rear-guard received all stragglers, and consisted of a body of Cossacks, a portion of the camp patrol, and the camels destined to carry the troops.

In order to allow the camels sufficient time for grazing, the columns always halted one or two hours before sunset. The camels were led to pasturage under a guard, consisting of a fourth of the whole number of Kirghizes and Cossacks in the column; the latter also did picket duty round the camp. Two or three sentries were stationed in front of each line of piled luggage, to prevent the Kirghizes opening the bales, which these "sons of the desert" were rather inclined to do. The

Cossack pickets, three men to each, were posted at the distance of a verst round the camp, to see that nobody stole in or out.

Towards dusk the camels were brought back from their pastures, and fastened up for the night in the camp. The officers called over their muster rolls of men and camels, and made their report to the commander of the column.

The first two days were very fine, almost without wind, and with 4° (R.) of frost; but on the 19th (31st) November a north-easterly wind began to blow, and the thermometer sank to 10° (R.). On the 21st December (2nd January) there was a slight fall of snow; and on the following day, when the columns reached Iletsk Zachita, there were 18° of frost in the morning and 29° towards evening.

Henceforward frosts and snowstorms accompanied the columns without intermission on the whole march. For those who had always lived in warm houses, and but rarely ventured out of doors in winter, except when hunting or performing short journeys, the frost during the first few days was intolerable; for it was, of course, impossible to dress as warmly when out campaigning on horseback as when travelling. At night the frost generally increased; "and sleeping on the frozen ground spread over with felt, under a felt tent, and even when rolled up in a sheepskin, is rather cold work." The men generally covered themselves from head to foot, to prevent their noses getting frost-bitten; but during the night, from the breathing and perspiration of the sleepers, the sheepskins froze to the hair of their heads and their moustaches, so that on getting up in the morning it took them considerable time to disentangle their hair from the sheepskin. During the first nights nobody could sleep because of the great frosts, but afterwards habit and nature triumphed. Frosts of 15° and 20° R. were at last regarded as comparative thaws, and, in spite of the cold, all slept soundly after a fatiguing day's march.

Fortunately, some of the men provided themselves on the halt at Iletz Zachita with iron stoves; and tents furnished with these proved of great service.

If it were possible to advance in the steppe without being exposed to chances of attack or loss of cattle from marauding Kirghizes, the most convenient and rapid mode of performing the march would be to adopt the order observed by the trade caravans. These advance in two or three lines, the detachment being divided into several small columns, each consisting of 800 or 1,000 camels, so as to allow each party, without preserving any particular order, to start in the morning as soon as the camels have been packed, and halt for the night at any point they may find most convenient. But in such a case it would be impossible to exercise any command over the whole detachment, and all military rules and precautions would necessarily have to be neglected.

It is evident that this manner of marching cannot be adopted by an expeditionary force despatched with military objects, which should be ready at any moment to repel an attack of the enemy from whatever quarter it might come, and which must therefore advance in such order as to be able to form a defensive encampment without loss of time.

It was necessary to plan an order of marching which should satisfy military requirements, and be at the same time of a simple character. Such a mode of advance was devised by the officers of the Staff of the Orenburg Corps. It was based on the consideration that the detachment consisted of troops who had never seen warfare, and who were accompanied by an enormous train, including more than 2,000 Kirghiz camel-drivers of doubtful loyalty, requiring strict supervision, unaccustomed to order and discipline, and ignorant of the Russian language; and that it was necessary to instruct the detachment in the order of march which would have to be observed on entering the dominion of Khiva. A campaign, therefore, at a short distance from the " Line" would have to serve as an experiment and as a model for the subsequent advance and deployment of the troops in the steppe.

In order to command the detachment with greater efficiency it would have been preferable to have allowed it to march in one body; but the advance and disposition in the steppe of a force consisting of more than 2,000 men and 9,000 camels presented the following drawbacks :—

1st. Large and good pasturage for the cattle and fuel for the men could not always be found at the halting-places. 2ndly. It would be necessary to graze the camels at a great distance from the camp, and consequently it would be more difficult and occupy more time to collect them. Moreover, as, during the winter days, only two or three hours were available for grazing, the cattle could not be driven far from camp. 3rdly. There were no established roads across the steppe. When crossing ravines, gullies, rivulets, and rivers it would not be always possible to advance with an extended front; all the columns would have to be contracted and drawn out into a long line, which would arrest the progress of each column for several hours. These delays, as it proved afterwards, would have been still greater had the force not been divided into columns; and consequently the horses and camels would have endured greater fatigue by standing for many hours with their loads on their backs. It was for these reasons, therefore, that the expeditionary force was divided into separate columns; and as it was known that the enemy was not distinguished for bravery, discipline, or knowledge of the military art, no serious danger was apprehended from such a division.

The detachment, as it was organised, resembled a large caravan or train, carrying with it a supply of material for the whole campaign, provisions for two months, and a large quantity of miscellaneous stores; which entailed the necessity of adapting its military organisation and campaigning arrangements to the order of march and of night halts observed by trains following the rear of armies.

The Russian expeditionary force being accompanied by a train so large as to include two camels to every combatant, could not advance in the same manner as, for instance, Bonaparte did in Egypt, where his trains were protected by being placed in the centre of squares, and where he was able to bring up his supplies along the Nile. Nor could the Russians adopt the plan pursued by the French in Algeria, where the troops are seldom moved more than 150 or 200 miles from the dépôts, and where, consequently, no necessity existed for taking large supplies for an expedition. Thus Bugeaud, in his celebrated movement preceding the battle of Isly, pushed forward only two short stages from the entrenched camp at Lalla-Magramia, where his dépôt of stores was concentrated. The supplies for 10,000 French troops, occupying a space of only 150 fathoms in length and twenty-five in breadth, could be easily protected by troops formed into battalion squares placed at short distances from each other.

The main column started from Bish Tamak on the 7th (19th) December in 30° (R.) of frost. The snow, owing to the cold, was crisp under foot. No bushes were now to be seen, and in the distance the summits of hillocks, covered with snow and brilliantly illuminated by the sun, could alone be distinguished. This brilliant reflection and the whiteness of the snow began to affect the sight of the men. The columns had scarcely gone seven or eight versts when, about noon, the sky became hidden in dense clouds, and a north-easterly wind sprang up, scattering clouds of snow, and soon attained the force of a " buran."

Beyond a distance of twenty yards no object could be seen through the clouds of snow which were whirled about in every direction. The fury of the storm was so great that it was impossible to draw breath when facing the wind, and the intense cold penetrated to the bones. The order of the advance could not be observed, and so as not to get lost in this fog of snow, the column was rapidly halted.

The " buran " lasted the whole night and subsided towards noon the next day. The Kirghizes said that if the snow had not been hardened previously by the frost, the tents would have been buried by the fall. There was a perceptible increase in the depth of the snow in the steppe after the storm ; and it was then, when it had to cross ravines and hollows drifted over with snow, that the detachment experienced all the hardships and fatigues of a winter steppe campaign.

Directly the *réveillé* sounded, preparations were set on foot for the resumption of the march. The piteous cries of the numerous camels upon being forced to rise on their feet, the neighing of horses, the babel of tongues—Kirghiz, Bashkir, Uralian and Russian all intermixed—blended into one wild discordant sound, which echoed far and wide over the steppe.

On the march from Iletz-Zachita to Fort Emba, that is from 22nd November (4th December) to the 21st December (2nd January), only once did the glass rise to 9° (R.), and this was by comparison considered a thaw. For eight days the frost ranged from 10° to 15° (R.), for six days from 25° to 30° (R.), while for three days it exceeded 30° (R.). These frosts were not unfrequently accompanied by a biting wind, which sometimes assumed the fury of a "buran."

The depth of the snow was increased by the snow-drifts, which daily augmented the difficulties of the march. The transport of the sick and of the six and twelve-pounder guns was attended with particular difficulty, as the wheels of the hospital carts and gun-carriages cut deep into the snow. The wheels were, however, taken off, and wooden slides fixed to the body of the carriage, by which means the difficulty was partially overcome. Along the whole distance, from the Orenburg Line to the River Emba, the columns did not see a single Kirghiz aúl, and it was only on the stage to Fort Emba that they passed some tents of Kirghizes of the Nazar tribe, near which were grazing large numbers of horses and sheep.

Taking advantage of this opportunity, 1,000 sheep were bought from the Kirghizes for the provisionment of the column, and a few fresh camels procured in lieu of those which had become exhausted.

At last, after a very tedious and fatiguing march down the valley of the Emba, along which only six or eight rows of camels could advance abreast, the column reached Fort Emba on the 19th (31st) December, where it found the detachment of Colonel Bizianov, who had already arrived from the Nijni Urulsk Line on the 9th (21st) December.

The whole march from Orenburg to Fort Emba, a distance of 472 versts, was performed by the detachment in thirty-two days. Not a single man had died from cold, although there were numerous cases of frost-bite.

CHAPTER VI.

PEROFSKI'S EXPEDITION *(continued)*.

THE four columns were disposed in four separate camps around the fortification, at a distance of from a half to one verst. As all the herbage about the fort was consumed, it became necessary to drive the camels to new pasture-grounds, at a distance of twenty-five versts. It was, moreover, desirable that the detachment should remain for a few days at the Emba fortification, to recruit its strength before encountering still greater fatigue, and in order that the weak and unserviceable camels might be picked out, and the packs of the stronger animals reduced to four or five poods each. The original packs of six or seven poods formed together a load of twelve to fourteen poods per camel, which was now too heavy for the exhausted beasts. It was also necessary to await the arrival of fresh camels, on their way to the Emba, and to prepare means of transport for the sick along the remaining distance to Khiva; a matter of no ordinary difficulty. The men disabled by sickness and disease had hitherto been transported partly in waggons and partly in sledges. Beyond the Emba, however, the great depth of the snow, the uneven character of the ground—holes and hollows occurring at almost every step—and the steep ascent to the Ust-Urt, involved the necessity of transporting the invalids on camels.

In Egypt and Algeria, where the only difficulty to contend with is the sultry heat, the arrangement of these invalid-packs is, according to the official writer, " comparatively easy." In the Egyptian campaign of Bonaparte boxes of five feet long were fixed to the packs, one end of the box opening on hinges, to allow the sick man to stretch out his legs when he wished. In Algeria, the French, during their expeditions into the desert, carry their sick on the backs of mules, in a kind of chair in which the sick man is strapped. The Russians could not adopt either of these methods, as the sick men might get frozen to death in severe weather. There remained only one method of conveying them: by means, that is to say, of a species of hammock, about six feet in length, filled with hay and wool, in which the sick were placed, wrapped warmly in felt. Although the hammocks thus prepared were not, perhaps, very comfortable to lie in, none of the sick were injured by frost. The strongest camels were selected for carrying them, and two hammocks were slung on each camel. Fortunately there was a person attached to the force who voluntarily assumed the duties of looking after the sick, and moving them to and from their hammocks. This benevolent man was Chichachef, the celebrated Russian traveller, who had received permission from the authorities to join the expedition as a looker-on. He intended, after reaching Khiva, to survey the sources of the Oxus and Jaxartes and the Pamir mountains; whence he proposed to return to Russia by way of Thibet and India.

During the whole progress of the march from the Line to the Emba fortification, the column had not been attacked either by the Kaisaks or by the Khivans. It had met no enemy. Reports had, it is true, been received of the collection of a considerable force of Khivans on the Syr-Daria (Jaxartes), at Karatamack (a bay on the north-western shore of the sea of Aral); but as these rumours had been in circulation for nearly six months, they were at last discredited altogether. Suddenly the commander of the Ak-Bulak fort reported that he had been attacked by the Khivans.

They had appeared near Fort Ak-Bulak on the 18th (30th) December, 2,000 or 3,000 strong, approaching at a brisk trot, and halting within one and a half versts of the fort. A body of their picked horsemen dashed off to attack the picket stationed at a short distance, but the soldiers had had time to retreat to the fort. At the same time the mounted Khivans divided themselves into several bodies, and made a simultaneous attack on the fortification from the eastern and northern sides. Fortunately a false alarm had been sounded the night before, when the men had been told off to their several quarters, and the officers appointed to their respective posts; consequently no confusion arose on the unexpected attack from the Khivans. Inside the fortress there were only 130 able-bodied men; but at the moment of danger 164 sick soldiers rose from their beds, seized their arms, and joined their comrades on the walls. The musketry and artillery fire, skilfully directed by two officers of Mining Engineers, repulsed the enemy with considerable loss.

Notwithstanding this, however, they continued their unsuccessful attacks until nightfall, forming, when out of gunshot, into new bodies, and then rushing forward to attack again, and harmlessly discharging their muskets at the garrison. Observing that some haystacks stood in front of the entrance to the fort on the western side, the Khivans repeatedly endeavoured to approach them, evidently with the intention of forcing their way into the fort under cover. They were, however, each time foiled in their attempts by the Cossacks and infantry soldiers who sallied out against them. In the night they attempted to set fire to the ricks, but in this they likewise failed.

The next day the enemy, having previously observed that there were no guns on one face of the fort, attacked it from that side; but overnight a barbette had been erected there, on which, during the attack, guns were hastily mounted, so that the Khivans, on making the attack, were dispersed with grape. After this failure they retired about three versts, and formed themselves into one body, ranged under their several banners. Hearing that a small Russian detachment was encamped at a short distance from the fort, the Khivans resolved to destroy it. This was the transport train that had been despatched for the removal of the sick and superfluous heavy articles from the Ak-Bulak to the River Emba, and which was at that time only one stage distant from the fortification. Being unaware of the proximity of the enemy, this detachment, under the command of Erofeyef, had halted at seventeen versts from Ak-Bulak. The camels and horses had been let loose to graze, and the men were employed in digging roots for fuel and in erecting the tents. While they were thus engaged the Khivan horsemen made a sudden appearance, but instead of immediately attacking the detachment, commenced driving away its horses and camels. This gave the Russians time to make a hasty entrenchment. Carts, sledges, and boxes were immediately formed into a temporary rampart, behind which the soldiers were placed to receive the enemy with discharges of musketry. The cavalry and infantry of the Khivans soon made successive charges on the camp, but were each time repulsed. At night the Khivans attempted to crawl up and take the Russians by surprise, but were driven off at the point of the bayonet and with musket shots. During the darkness, however, the Khivans succeeded in digging rifle-pits and throwing up earthworks at a distance of fifty yards on the four faces of the Russian camp; and they opened fire from these in the morning. From this position, however, they were soon dislodged; and seeing the futility of continuing their open attacks, they collected the horses and camels they had seized and drove them straight before them on to the Russian encampment, in the hope of being able to approach the camp safely under shelter of the animals. But Captain Erofeyef, divining their intention, detached twenty-five riflemen with orders to take up a position which would deprive the assailants of protection behind the horses and camels. This was skilfully executed, and the well-directed fire of the riflemen created confusion among the enemy. A sally was at the same time made from the camp, and the Khivans were beaten off with loss, leaving their dead behind, and losing a portion of the camels and horses previously seized from the Russians. Seeing the great loss they had sustained in men, and the utter failure of their attacks against the camp, the Khivans had now recourse to another stratagem. Two of their horsemen galloped up within gunshot and endeavoured to induce the Tartars and Kirghizes in the Russian service to join them, promising them favours and rewards if they did so, and threatening dire vengeance if they refused. "A few shots," we are told, "soon put an end to their persuasive eloquence."

The whole Khivan forces retired soon afterwards and were not seen or heard of again for a long while. The Russians subsequently ascertained that they had lost the greater part of their horses from the frost, many of the riders also falling victims to the severity of the winter. Out of the whole of this mass of 2,000 or 3,000 men—which had been commanded by the Kush Begi, or Minister of War—scarcely half returned to Khiva, and those were in a very sorry plight.

The exhortations and threats of the Khivans did not at the time produce the slightest effect on the Kirghizes, who were witnesses of their cowardice and defeat. But later on the exaggerated reports disseminated among the Kirghizes of the steppe by the Khivans respecting the strength of their forces and their reinforcement by an army of Kokandians, the threats of the Khan of Khiva, and religious fanaticism, stimulated and inflamed by Khivan emissaries, excited the Kirghiz camel-drivers to such an extent that on one occasion they collected together to the number of about 200, and refused to proceed any further. This disorderly crowd, in spite of all entreaties, refused to disperse, and, increasing in numbers, "disturbed the camp with their wild shouts and violent behaviour." It was necessary to adopt severe measures so as to save the detachment from being left in the heart of the frozen steppe, at a distance of 500 versts from the Line, without any means of locomotion. The crowd was surrounded by troops, and after two of the ringleaders had been shot, the malcontents dispersed, and resumed their duties.

While the main detachment lay encamped at the Emba, a report was received that, the supplies of provisions despatched in vessels to Novo-Alexandrofsk having been delayed at sea by contrary winds until late in the autumn, ten of the ships had become fixed in the ice, some in sight of Fort Alexandrofsk, and some within 100 versts of Gurief, near the Prorvinsk islands. It was further stated that only two of the vessels had succeeded in returning to Astrakhan, after sustaining considerable injury and losing part of their cargoes, which the crew were compelled to throw overboard.

Owing to the exertions of the commandant of

Novo-Alexandrofsk, the vessels frozen in the ice near that fort were saved, and their cargoes brought on shore. Those transports, however, which were wedged in the ice near Prorvinsk Post were burnt by Turcomans and Kirghizes sent thither for the purpose by the Khivans.

While at Emba some of the soldiers were exercised in making night signals by the ignition of gunpowder—in which manner all communications were correctly maintained between the columns—others practised firing with shot and shell; and experiments were successfully made in exploding mines under the ice by means of a galvanic battery.

The distance between the Emba fortification and Ak-Bulak by the direct winter route did not exceed 160 versts, and it was traversed by the columns in fifteen days. Notwithstanding this, however, the loss in camels was very great, and continued to increase daily. The detachment, when it crossed the Line, had about 10,000 camels. But after passing Fort Emba, it could with difficulty muster 8,900 camels for transporting provisions and provender for two months; while at Ak-Bulak, a point not even half-way to Khiva, the number of serviceable camels had been reduced to 5,188. The number that actually died between the Emba and Ak-Bulak was only 1,200; the rest being abandoned on the road on account of their complete exhaustion.

To render the march of the unloaded camels less fatiguing, the infantry columns advanced in front of them, in four files, forming beaten tracks in the snow; the advance of the loaded camels being assisted in the same way by the cavalry. Where the snow was very deep, the cavalry passed and repassed several times over the ground, to enable the camels to proceed without any difficulty. In some parts the snow was even shovelled away by the soldiers; but in spite of all this the camels continued to fall in great numbers, thus obstructing the advance of the columns. When a camel succumbed it was necessary to remove its load; and the men sinking to their knees, and sometimes to their waists, in snow, exhausted their strength in this labour. When a camel fell it rarely rose again, so that new paths had to be made round this obstruction for the passage of camels following in the rear.

The guns had to be drawn by horses, and occasionally to be pulled out of the snow by the men. In some places the surface of the snow was quite soft, while in others it was nearly as hard as ice, and supported the horses, camels, and even the 12-pounder guns. At times, when it gave way, the extrication of the camels, sledges, artillery, and so on, was attended with great fatigue and difficulty. The camels and horses got cut about the legs, and on some days only short stages of four versts were made in consequence of these delays. In " burans," or snow-storms, it was altogether impossible to advance. Thus the first column, which marched during a snow-storm, was only able to traverse twenty versts in four days; and it abandoned on the road a large number of sledges and carts, which the following three columns converted into fuel for cooking purposes.

After such severe frost and such fatiguing stages, the strength of the camels should have been recruited with plentiful food. But the surface of the steppe—poor at any time—was now completely covered with snow. It was, however, still possible to give each horse a measure of oats and about five pounds of hay per diem; although to feed 8,000 camels on hay was, of course, not feasible. The latter, however, were each apportioned about five pounds of hay a day; which was little enough.

It must be added that the frost, during this time,

was 15° and 20° R.; and, although the men had to a certain extent become acclimatised, the great cold benumbed their limbs, in spite of their warm clothing, and incapacitated them for all work. "At the same time," says the official writer, "hard work—producing perspiration, exhaustion, and sound sleep—exposed the men to the liability of catching cold."

For the first eighty versts the columns marched along the left banks of the Arty Takshi, and then followed the course of the Talysai rivulet, proceeding afterwards across saline marshes, which the frost rendered firm ground in winter, thus enabling the camels, horses, and artillery to cross without any difficulty. During summer, draught horses sink here up to their fetlocks in the oozy mud, and the wheels of carts laden with goods become embedded a foot deep. After a fall of rain, however, or during spring, it is altogether impossible to cross these saline-marsh tracts, which extend to Chushka-Kul, over a distance of eighty versts. They are intersected by two ranges of hills—the Bakzir and Ali—over which there are convenient ascents and descents for vehicles. But along the whole of this marshy tract a plentiful supply of good water is only to be found on the slope of the Ali hills; the pasturage for cattle throughout the distance being, moreover, poor and scanty. In consequence of frost and snow, and scarcity of fuel, it took the column six or seven days to traverse these salines, and it was on these stages that they encountered the difficulties described above.

General Perofski, who had remained with a light detachment at Fort Emba to superintend the departure of the last column, and to make proper arrangements for the safety and requirements of the sick left behind, quitted the Fort on the 17th (29th) January, and after inspecting the column which he overtook on the march, went forward to Ak-Bulak to make arrangements for the further advance of the troops. On reaching Ak-Bulak, he immediately despatched Colonel Bizianof and Captain Rechenberg, with 150 Ural Cossacks and one light field gun, to reconnoitre the route ahead, and to find a convenient point of ascent to the Ust-Urt. This detachment, after going 150 versts in the direction of Khiva, returned eight days later, reporting that the depth of snow for 100 versts, as far as the Ust-Urt, was still greater than that on the steppe already traversed; that the grass and bushes were buried in snow, and that some parts of the route were so blocked with snow that they could with difficulty be passed even by horses. On the Ust-Urt, along which Colonel Bizianof advanced twenty versts, there was less snow than below; but even there the quantity was unusually great. No traces of the enemy were to be discovered anywhere, from which it was justly concluded that the Khivans had marched homewards in consequence of the extraordinary severity of the winter.

Some account of their partial operations against the Russians is given by Captain Abbott in the narrative of his mission to Khiva, which he reached from Herat, by way of Merv, at the very time when Perofski was advancing towards Khiva from Orenburg. The Khivan horsemen complained that, in consequence of the severe cold, they were unable to handle their matchlocks with effect; while the Russians, they said, kept their hands warm by means of their camp-fires.

Meanwhile the third, or main column, of the Russian force, comprising the park of artillery, reached Ak-Bulak on the 25th February (6th March), 1840; sixteen days after its departure from Fort Emba. Although this column had been preceded by the two foremost columns, and had left only six days after the second one, it was, in some places, obliged to clear a new route for itself, the tracks and trodden paths of the columns in advance having become drifted over with snow. Only now and then could the route taken by the columns in front be ascertained through the pillars of snow erected at some distance from each other by the Ural Cossacks, through the snow-heaps which marked the night camps, and through the camels, living and dead, some frozen and partly devoured by wild beasts, that lay along the line of march.

If the passage of Macdonald's corps, 12,000 strong, in 1800, over the Simplon, be justly considered a wonderful feat on account of the extraordinary exertions of the French, and the great hardships to which they were exposed, how much higher, asks the official historian, must we place the endurance and discipline of the Russian troops, who encountered difficulties immeasurably greater on their march through the deep snows from Emba to Ak-Bulak, during frosts, storms, and hurricanes of unprecedented severity, and over a desert and frozen tract of 160 versts (107 miles), the advance lasting a period of half a month?

After marching in hard frosts a distance of 500

versts through an inhospitable steppe covered with deep snow, and after a short halt at Fort Emba, which did not, however, afford the men any rest owing to the heavy labour they had to perform there, the troops had further to advance across a steppe still more barren and inhospitable. It was found necessary to clear the way for the 6,000 camels through the deep snow-drifts; and the men had very often to work up to their waists in snow during a frost of 20° R., adjusting the packs, loading and unloading them, and so on. The unfortunate camels had become so weak from fatigue, insufficient food, and cold, that even the Kirghiz drivers, who rarely walk, did not mount them for several stages before Ak-Bulak, but proceeded on foot. A new source of anxiety appeared on the march to Ak-Bulak. The famished camels gnawed the bark boxes and matting sacks, in order to get at the biscuits, flour, and corn they contained; and pulled the compressed hay out of the bundles. In this manner more of the stores were wasted than eaten by the camels, and it was consequently necessary to keep a strict watch over them, and at once repair any damage done to the packs. At each halting-place 19,000 packages had to be unloaded and again loaded. Before a fire could be lit, the materials for it, consisting usually of small roots of shrubs, had to be picked out of the hard and frozen ground. Spaces had to be cleared of snow for the tents, camels, &c. ; and it was only towards 8 or 9 o'clock in the evening that the soldier or Cossack could obtain a little repose, while by 2 or 3 o'clock the next morning he was obliged to rise and go through the same round of heavy duties.

When the detachment arrived at Ak-Bulak the frost had increased to 30° R.

During this cold weather, on clear days, columns of the colours of the rainbow were often visible at sunrise in the sky; and on other occasions "two suns appeared shining at the sides of the true luminary with almost equal brilliancy."

In such frost it was impossible to wash linen or observe personal cleanliness. Many of the men during the whole campaign not only did not change their linen, but did not even take off their clothes. They were of course covered with vermin, and their bodies became ingrained with dirt and predisposed to disease.

General Perofski left the Emba fortification on the 17th (29th) Jan. with a small Cossack detachment, and having overtaken the last two columns on the route to Ak-Bulak, was personally an eye-witness of the hardships endured by the troops on the march. He saw, too, the complete exhaustion of the camels. Observing the position in which the expeditionary force was placed, the General sought the opinion of the commanders of the columns as to the possibility of their camels reaching Khiva. The commanders reported that, owing to the wearied condition of these animals, the scantiness of herbage, and the great depth of snow on the ground, any further advance towards Khiva was impossible. The same opinion was confirmed by the ruler of the western horde, the Sultan Aichuvakof, who, as a Kirghiz, was well acquainted both with the powers of endurance of the camel, and the condition of the steppe. Besides procuring the opinion of the commanders of the columns and of the Sultan Aichuvakof, General Perofski, on reaching Ak-Bulak, despatched Colonel Bizianof to the Ust-Urt, as already stated, with the Ural Cossacks, to examine the route in front. Then, having found that the depth of the snow became greater and greater, that all herbage and fuel were completely buried under it, and that the weakness of the camels, which were beginning to fall at the rate of a hundred daily, increased from hour to hour, he became convinced that it was impossible, under the circumstances to reach Khiva.

The Orenburg infantry soldiers, not being accustomed to the fatigues of a campaign, suffered severely from disease. On the completion of half the journey only 1,856 effective men could be mustered out of a force of 2,750 which had left Orenburg. Of the number on the sick list, 236 had already died, 528 remained under treatment, and 130 were invalided and left behind at Fort Emba. On reaching Khiva the number of sick would in all probability be still greater.

"If," says the official writer, "the mortality and exhaustion among the camels were to go on increasing at the same rate, which in all probability it would do, the detachment would be obliged to return to Fort Emba before reaching Khiva, after abandoning its provisions and stores on the route, and encountering still greater difficulties than those already experienced. And, furthermore, if the enemy were at this juncture to commence marching to meet the Russians, might not the return of the latter be interpreted as a flight from the advancing enemy? In every case, therefore, it was preferable to succumb to the insurmountable obstacles of nature, and to retreat at once, than to give the miserable enemies of the Russians any pretext for exultation over an imaginary victory."

All these reasons convinced General Perofski of the impossibility of continuing the march to Khiva, and reconciled him to the sad necessity of returning to Fort Emba, where there was a stock of provisions calculated to last the detachment until spring.

On the 1st of February General Perofski issued the following order to the troops :—

" Comrades ! It will soon be three months since we commenced our march with a sincere trust in God and a firm resolution to fulfil the orders of our Emperor. Ever since we started we have had to struggle against obstacles of the most formidable character, and a winter of unprecedented severity. These difficulties we have successfully overcome ; but we have not had the satisfaction of meeting the enemy, and the only slight collision we had with him showed his contemptible inferiority. In spite of all the fatigue you have endured, you are still full of energy and vigour. The horses are in good condition, and our supplies are plentiful. In one thing only have we been unfortunate; we have lost a large proportion of our camels, and those remaining are exhausted by hunger and fatigue. We are thus deprived of the means of transporting our stores of provisions for the remaining distance along the route. However painful it may be to forego the victory that awaited us, we must on this occasion retrace our steps towards the frontier. There we shall await the further orders of the Emperor. Our next expedition will be more fortunate. It is a source of consolation for me to be able to thank you for the unflagging devotion and energy which you have displayed under all the difficulties encountered on the march. Our gracious Sovereign and Father shall know it all."

According to calculations made afterwards, it appeared that from the day of the departure of the detachment to the 20th February, the number of sick cases, both in the marching columns and fort garrisons, amounted to 3,124, out of which 608 were fatal.

The following was the ratio of sickness and deaths among the different branches of the expeditionary force :—

	Ratio of Sickness.	Ratio of Deaths.
Orenburg Infantry	1 to 2	1 to 14
Detachment of 1st Orenburg Regiment	1 to 2 and 3	1 to 26
Orenburg Cossacks	1 to 4 and 5	1 to 34
Ural Cossacks	1 to 27	1 to 200

These figures show that the Orenburg infantry troops were the worst, and the Ural Cossacks the best qualified for campaigning in the steppe.

Of the 10,500 camels with which the expeditionary force had been supplied at starting, only 1,500 remained alive on the 13th April. At the same date the number of sick in the camps amounted to 7 civil officials and 853 soldiers. The number of deaths up to the 14th March was 761, comprising three civil officials and 758 officers and men. The numerical strength of the force encamped on the Saga-Temir river consisted of 86 superior and subaltern officers, and 2,895 men. From the commencement of the campaign to the 4th May, the total mortality in the expeditionary force amounted to 80 officers of various kinds and 800 soldiers.

In the summer expedition to Khiva of Prince Bekovitch in 1717, a quarter of the men died on the march; while in the winter campaign of General

Perofski in 1839, the mortality among the whole force employed reached about one-third. These two experiments would seem to testify in favour of summer expeditions in the steppe. Seeing that the country traversed by General Perofski yielded an abundant supply of water, the commencement of the campaign in winter was decidedly unadvisable. The whole force might have been collected on the Ust-Urt before winter set in.

There were many officers who condemned the plan of a winter campaign when it was in contemplation; but the opinions of those who supported their arguments to the contrary by quoting Lord Wellington's saying, that "Sandy wastes can only be traversed by troops in winter," preponderated.

As soon as it became known that the first expeditionary force would not be able to reach Khiva, orders were issued for strengthening the Orenburg Corps with six battalions. Admiral Rimski Korsakof was sent to ascertain the number of vessels on the Volga and Caspian capable of transporting these troops to the eastern coast of the Caspian, in order that Khiva might be reached by the route taken by Prince Bekovitch. When it was found that there were not sufficient vessels available, it was decided to follow the same route as that which had already proved so disastrous to the recent expedition; but with this difference, that the troops should be concentrated in the steppe early in the autumn, so that they might only have the Ust-Urt to march across during the winter.

No fresh expedition, however, was undertaken; and the pretext on which General Perofski had based his meditated attack upon Khiva no longer existed. As if to deprive the Russians of all excuse for making war upon the Khan, two English officers, Captain Abbott and Captain Shakespear, sent from India on a mission to Khiva, had, at the very time General Perofski was advancing, procured the liberation of the Russian prisoners; who, after terms had been arranged by Abbott, were escorted by Shakespear to their native land.

The Russians now left Khiva alone, until the year 1858, when Colonel, now General, Ignatieff, formerly ambassador at Constantinople, afterwards Minister of the Interior at St. Petersburg, undertook a diplomatic mission on so large a scale that it had almost the character of a military expedition. Meanwhile, however, a definite arrangement in regard to the Central Asian question had been come to between England and Russia.

CHAPTER VII.

THE ANGLO-RUSSIAN AGREEMENT OF 1844.

WHEN, in 1844, the Emperor Nicholas started for England in order to visit Queen Victoria he was convinced that the only stumbling-block between England and Russia was the apprehension caused to the former by the ambitious views attributed to the latter in the East. He resolved then to see the English Sovereign and the English Ministers on this subject; ready to give, in regard not only to Turkey, but also Central Asia, all needful explanations and all possible guarantees. Perofski's expedition to Khiva in 1839, following immediately after the siege of Herat, which had been conducted by Russian engineers under the direction of a Russian general, had, in spite of its disastrous result, caused much speculation, some apprehension, and, among a small party, downright alarm. Every Russian sovereign, from Peter the Great to Paul, and, in our own century, from Paul to Alexander I., and from Alexander I. to Nicholas, was known to have entertained designs against India; and the notion that Russia at Khiva would be a menace to India was entertained in England by a select party of "alarmists"—among whom Her Majesty's Ministers were included—as long ago as 1840; immediately, that is to say, after the news of Perofski's expedition against Khiva reached England. In regard to Central Asia, as in regard to Turkey, the Emperor Nicholas was ready to give assurances of his friendly intentions towards England, all that he demanded in return being a loyal adherence to the *status quo* in Europe; which of course implied abandonment of the French alliance and a friendly agreement with Russia.

In 1844, then, the Emperor Nicholas went to England, visited Queen Victoria, and had numerous interviews with Lord Aberdeen, who was at that time Foreign Minister. As to the future, he was prepared to give the most distinct pledges; and on his return to St. Petersburg he directed Count Nesselrode, Minister of Foreign Affairs, to draw up a memorandum based on what had passed between him and Lord Aberdeen during his stay in London.

The memorandum is given at length in the *"Diplomatic Study on the Crimean War,"* issued by the Russian Foreign Office; and it is probably to this document that Mr. Thornton refers in his *"Lives of English Foreign Secretaries,"* as one which, without having been placed in the archives of our Foreign Office, was handed from minister to minister at each change of Government. However that may be, the memorandum must be accepted as reproducing in substance the agreement come to between the Emperor Nicholas and the Government of England in the year 1844; and it throws a new light, to the advantage of the Emperor Nicholas, on the celebrated conversation which he held nine years afterwards with Sir Hamilton Seymour on the subject of the "Sick Man." The objects with which, in case of "anything happening" to the Sick Man, Russia and England would have to come to an understanding, were set forth as follows :—

" 1. Maintenance of the Ottoman Empire for so long a time as this political combination may be possible.

" 2. If we see beforehand that it is breaking up, a preliminary understanding to be arrived at as to the establishment of a new order of things destined to replace that which now exists; and precautions to be taken in common, so that no change occurring in the internal situation of that empire may threaten the security of our own states, or the maintenance of the European equilibrium.

"In view of the objects thus formulated, the policy of Russia and that of Austria are clearly bound together by the principle of complete solidarity. If England, as the chief naval power, acts in concert with them, there is reason to believe that France will find herself obliged to follow the course decided upon between St. Petersburg, London, and Vienna. All possibility of conflict between the Great Powers being thus averted, it may be hoped that the peace of Europe will be maintained, even in the midst of such grave circumstances.

"It is with the view of assuring this result in the interests of all, that Russia and England should first come to a preliminary understanding between themselves, as agreed upon by the Emperor with the Ministers of her Britannic Majesty during his stay in England."

Viewed in connection with this memorandum, addressed in 1844 by the Russian Government to the Government of England, and accepted by the latter, the conversation of the Emperor Nicholas with Sir Hamilton Seymour in 1853 acquires a new character. The "Sick Man," whose introduction to the world through the published despatches of Sir Hamilton Seymour caused so much scandal at the time of the Crimean war, was but a revival. He is at least foreshadowed, with the mortal character of his malady already indicated, in those clauses of the Nesselrode Memorandum which consider the probability of "something happening" to Turkey, and which stipulate that on the occurrence of the unhappy event, England and Russia shall come to an understanding, with a view to action in common.

But England in 1844 mistrusted Russia, in connection not only with Turkey but also with Central Asia. Apart from Perofski's expedition to Khiva, of which the immediate effect, even in case of success, could only have told indirectly and remotely upon India, Russia had helped the Persians during the siege of Herat with money, arms and men, and she had been intriguing against us in Afghanistan; a fact better known to the English Government, who had received particulars on the subject from its agents at Cabul, than to the English public, to whom the despatches from these agents were presented in a mutilated form, with almost everything that compromised Russia cut out. The Emperor Nicholas, however, must have been aware that the offers of arms and money made on his part by the Polish agent, Captain Vitkievitch, to Dost Mohamed, had become known to us through the reports of Burnes and others. It was a matter of European notoriety, moreover, that the Persian force which had laid siege to Herat had been commanded by a Russian, General Barofsky—confounded by some of our agents in Cabul with the Perofski of the Khivan expedition; and to leave nothing unsettled between the two countries, the Emperor Nicholas proposed an agreement on the subject of Central Asia as well as Turkey.

Already the idea of a "neutral zone" was entertained; a geographical and political idea, which, far from remaining fixed, shifts its ground constantly, and always to move in the direction of India. In 1844, for example, Russia agreed "to leave the Khanates of Central Asia as a neutral zone interposed between the two empires, so as to preserve them from dangerous contact." In 1869 the zone which by the agreement of that year was to be regarded as "beyond the interference of Russia," consisted of Afghanistan proper and the little states of Afghan Turkestan, between the Hindu-Kush and the Oxus. The possibility of leaving Afghan Turkestan untouched, and the propriety of advancing the Russian frontier to the Hindu-Kush is now, both by Russian officers and Russian publicists, being actively discussed. By the secret convention, or interchanged memorandum, however, of 1844, not only did Russia engage to leave independent the Khanates of Khiva, Bokhara, and Khokand, but she also agreed with England to take general measures for assuring the peace of Persia, and in particular " for forestalling the dangers of a contested succession and for regulating in common the frontier relations on the one side with Turkey, on the other with Afghanistan."

The remarks made by the author of the official "*Diplomatic Study on the Crimean War,*" in regard to Central Asia and Persia, are very strange. " Faithfully observed by Russia, this programme," he says, " preserved the tranquillity of Asia for twenty years ; " that is to say, until 1864, in which year General Tchernaieff interfered rudely enough both with Khokand and with Bokhara. But Lord Palmerston, we are told, " had broken the agreement on the subject, just as he had broken the one relating to Turkey "—for the Russian Foreign Office persists in its belief that Lord Palmerston was the true author of the Crimean war. Immediately after the Treaty of 1856 he " profited by circumstances to wage war against Persia, in order to make that country feel the power of Great Britain, and to take from it definitively Herat, which was then annexed to Afghanistan." " Thence," it is added, " resulted the progress since accomplished in Central Asia by Russia restored to her full liberty of action, and free from all illusions as to the utility of subordinating her interests to the idea of an impossible solidarity."

Whatever, then, English writers and English politicians may say on the subject, the Russians themselves have always regarded their movement towards Afghanistan as injurious to the interests of England. It is not astonishing that they should do so now, considering that the Emperor Nicholas took the same view in 1844, when not one successful step in that direction had as yet been made.

CHAPTER VIII.

IGNATIEFF'S MISSION TO KHIVA AND BOKHARA.

COUNT NICHOLAS PAVLOVITCH IGNATIEFF, who first owed his European fame to his restless activity as Ambassador of Russia at Constantinople, during and immediately before the recent Russo-Turkish war, is the son of the General Ignatieff who was for many years Governor-General of St. Petersburg, and who was afterwards President of the Committee of Ministers. Nicholas Pavlovitch Ignatieff was educated at the Institute of Pages, and, according to custom, quitted that select establishment to enter the Guards. The so-called "Crimean War" found the young Ignatieff, at the age of 22, serving with his regiment at Revel, in the Baltic provinces, under Count Berg, to whose staff he was attached. In spite of the exertions she was compelled to make in the Crimea, Russia, throughout the war of 1854 and 1855, kept her best troops in the neighbourhood of the capital, or else along the coast from which the capital might have been approached. The object, then, of the force stationed at Revel was to prevent the enemy from landing; and as the enemy did not land, it might be argued that this object was attained. Towards the end of the war Ignatieff followed his general to Finland, where Count Berg was soon afterwards appointed to the Governorship; a post he retained until 1863, when, at the height of the insurrection, he was sent as Governor to Poland.

Meanwhile, Captain Ignatieff had passed from the military to the diplomatic service, finding his point of transition in the post of Military Attaché to the Embassy at London.

His chief performance as Military Attaché to the Embassy of Baron Brunow was a careful report on England's military position in India, which so pleased the Emperor that His Majesty called the writer to Warsaw for a personal interview. It would be interesting to know whether Captain Ignatieff already foresaw the probability of the mutiny so soon afterwards to break out; and whether it was the method and style of the report, or its substance and the views enunciated therein, which commended it to the attention of Alexander II. Doubtless the latter. But Russian diplomacy keeps its secrets; and in no Russian Blue-book has Captain Ignatieff's report on England's military position in India been published.

In 1858 Ignatieff, now a Colonel, was sent on a special mission to Khiva and Bokhara. The mission might equally have been called a reconnoissance; and it was not without reason that its direction was entrusted to a diplomatist who had been a soldier.

In the year 1857 the Khans of Khiva and Bokhara had sent envoys to congratulate Alexander II. on his accession to the throne; and the Russian Government resolved to profit by the opportunity thus naturally presenting itself to renew communications with its ferocious neighbours, hitherto so difficult of access and so inhospitable when approached. Only sixteen years before, Colonel Stoddard and Captain Conolly, accredited agents of the British Government, had been executed at Bokhara; and seven years later Mr. Struvé, a diplomatic agent sent by General Tchernaieff to Bokhara, was thrown into prison by the Ameer, subjected to a variety of cruelties, and detained in captivity for six months; and that almost within sight of the Russian troops.

The journey, moreover, to Khiva presented difficulties which, in the case of a large force, had hitherto been found insurmountable. General Perofski in his expedition to Khiva of the year 1839 lost, as has been told at length, the greater part of his army through frost and snow; yet he had deliberately resolved to run all the hazards of a merciless winter season rather than attempt to march troops across the Ust-Urt desert in summer.

Ignatieff, however (now Colonel and Aide-de-camp to the Emperor), who had been entrusted with the leadership and direction of the mission, determined to start from Orenburg in summer; and, as he returned in the depth of winter, he is the one commander on whom the winds of the Ust-Urt desert have blown both hot and cold.

Ignatieff after his mission to Khiva was sent to China, where he concluded a very important treaty, by which the extensive and valuable province of Ussuri was ceded to Russia. During the occupation of Pekin by the French and English, he is said to have shown great tact in bringing to bear upon the Chinese his influence with the allies, and upon the allies his influence with the Chinese.

Returning to Russia, he was made Director of the Asiatic Department in the Ministry of Foreign

Affairs; a department in which, for no visible reason, Slavonic questions are treated. Here he drew up a plan for uniting the Orenburg and Siberian lines; afterwards executed by Colonel Verevkin, marching from Orenburg, and Colonel (now General) Tchernaieff marching from Semipalatinsk. He had previously urged upon the Government the necessity of occupying Tashkend, when he received the same answer which was afterwards given to Tchernaieff—that the Russian Government did not wish to extend its possessions in Central Asia, and that Tashkend was not to be taken.

It was thought that General Ignatieff would be made Governor-General of the Russian possessions in Central Asia. But in 1865 he was appointed minister at Constantinople, where his legation was subsequently raised to the rank of an embassy.

From London his report on the government of India seems to have taken him to Central Asia; his successes in Central Asia took him to China; his success in China to the direction of the Asiatic department where Slavonic affairs are treated. From the Asiatic department he was moved to Constantinople — the one point at which a true Russian of the orthodox faith is always stationed;

M

to the exclusion of the Baltic and other Germans who would not, it seems to be held, sympathise sufficiently with the oppressed Christians of the orthodox faith.

To speak now in detail of Ignatieff's Central Asian mission; which, as has already been seen, assumed the character of a return visit to visits made, on the occasion of the Emperor Alexander's accession to the throne, by ambassadors from the Khans of Khiva and Bokhara. The envoy from Khiva made his appearance at Orenburg on the 20th of July, 1857, bringing two argamaks as a gift to the Imperial Court, and attended by a suite of sixteen men. A house was hired for the accommodation of the mission. The envoy himself was allowed two roubles a day, while the other distinguished Khivans were paid seventy-five copecks (100 copecks to the rouble), and the rest twenty-five copecks.

The sensation created in Orenburg by the arrival of the Khivan Mission had not yet subsided, when a report from Orsk acquainted the authorities with the arrival at that fort, on the 10th (22nd) of August, of an envoy from Bokhara, with four argamaks and a suite of forty men. This suite represented a variety of offices and grades. There was the Commandant of the Bokharian Court; there were councillors and secretaries of embassy; adjutants, provosts, a guard of honour, grooms, a piper, a drummer, a doorkeeper, and four valets, the whole constituting a complete retinue. This company was likewise conveyed to Orenburg. Houses were hired, and another allowance of money was provided: two roubles to the envoy, one rouble twenty-five copecks to the commandant, and as much to the councillor; fifty copecks per man to eight "distinguished men," and twenty-five copecks to each of the rest. For every one of their horses they were furnished daily with two garnetz of oats and sixteen pounds of hay.

Having rested from the fatigues of their long journeys, the envoys, according to custom, asked to be allowed to proceed to the Imperial Court, in order to deliver the letters from the rulers of Khiva and Bokhara, and from their different ministers; declaring that the object of their missions was to offer congratulations to the Emperor on his happy accession to the throne of his forefathers.

In the letter from the Khan of Khiva there was, indeed, no mention of anything besides this; but in the letters from the Khivan ministers a unanimous desire was expressed to make the Jaxartes the boundary line between the territories of Khiva and the empire of Russia.

The contents of the letter from the ruler of Bokhara were of a different kind. Commencing with condolence on the death of the Emperor Nicholas, and congratulating his successor on his accession to the throne, the Ameer held it to be indispensably necessary at the same time to announce his victories in Shahr-i-Suby, and with the solemnity of a great monarch to make known his occupation of the little towns in that province, which lie within an area of from ten to twelve square versts. In conclusion, the Ameer expressed a desire to see a Russian envoy at Bokhara. "The intelligence," he wrote, "concerning the removal of the great sovereign from this perishable world to an eternal life, and the succession of the great monarch to the imperial throne reached our ears at the time when our most sacred person was engaged in the conquest of the Shahr-Kish dominions. Thanks to the Almighty and to His mercy, and owing to the efficacy of the prayers of the holy of the famous kingdom, the zephyr of victory and glory blew, and by the inexhaustible grace and lavish munificence of the Creator, the dominion of Shahr-Kish, Kital, Utra-kirgan, and Shamatan, with all their surrounding districts, have been overcome and subjected to the authority of the all-conquering kingdom.

" Owing to these causes, it has been made a matter of obligation to send an embassy to pray for the soul of the renowned Sovereign, to congratulate the monarch whose merits are equal to those of Dyemohidi, on his accession to the throne, and to make joyful communication of the conquest of the above-mentioned dominions. It is also despatched for the purpose of strengthening those bonds which have existed since the times of our ancestors, and of consolidating the mutual relations between two great sovereigns. We have, therefore, commanded the departure, as ambassador, of our respected and esteemed Mirakhur Mulladjan, a well-wisher to your Majesty, who is reputed among our nobles for his straightforwardness and justice. When vouchsafed a gracious reception we hope he will receive various imperial favours, and that his assurances will be kindly listened to ; after which we trust he will be granted permission to depart. May the precious and bright intelligence of the Sovereign be then directed towards the sending of an embassy from himself.

"Nothing is desired besides this; and so may the road to friendship and to mutual relations between the two great empires be open, enabling the caravans and traders of the two countries to come and go freely. As a token of remembrance we send a carpet of Cashmere manufacture, two Rezai-meshkin shawls, and a pair of black and piebald horses.

"May the sun of majesty eternally shine within the confines of the empire.

"Furthermore, greeting to him who follows the truth."

There is very little said of the Khivan envoy in the records of the period. All that can be gathered about him personally is that he was sparing of his words. But as regards the envoy from Bokhara, the following account was given by Mr. Gregorieff, the eminent Orientalist of the Asiatic Department of the Russian Foreign Office:—" Mulladjan Ashurdjanoff, who is styled Mir Akhur, *i.e.*, Master of the Horse, in the Ameer's letter to his Imperial Majesty, and in the letter from the Bokharian Ministers, did not fill that distinguished office at the Court of the Ameer, and must have received the title only on his appointment as Ambassador to the Court of Russia. Up to then he had held the post of Mir

Sheb, or night-policeman in the city of Bokhara, and in no way enjoyed the confidence of the Ameer Nasr Ullah. The councillor and the secretary of embassy are likewise persons who do not perform the duties which in Europe belong to those offices. The envoy treats them more like servants than like officials of a certain standing. A few days ago, finding them asleep when he awoke, he became furious, and with his own hand thrashed them with a *nagaika* (the Cossack horse-whip), and also laid it over the back of his son, the Commandant of the Bokharian Court."

Explaining further that the envoy was inquisitive, and that he readily entered into conversation about his own country, Mr. Gregorieff adds:—" He is very miserly, and consequently must be covetous, like all Asiatics. In proof of this, he refuses to provide his suite, at his own cost, with the warm clothing they require for their journey to St. Petersburg at this late season of the year; in consequence of which, by command of the Governor-General, the councillor and the secretary of the embassy have been supplied with pelisses, and the servants with tulups (sheep-skin coats), at the expense of our Government."

Such were the personages who, at that time, appeared in Russia as the representatives of Khiva and Bokhara.

On news being received at St. Petersburg of the arrival of the envoys, the imperial sanction was given for their admission to Court. On the 9th of September the Khivan envoy started for St. Petersburg, followed on the 23rd of October by the Bokharian envoy, accompanied by a limited suite.

Their stay in St. Petersburg was not long. Having been favoured with audiences, they received answers to the letters from their Khans and ministers; and after seeing ballets and other sights, and having, in particular, accumulated a good supply of presents, they returned to Orenburg in the month of January, 1858. From there they started for their respective countries; the Khivan envoy on the 28th of February, and the Bokharian envoy on the 24th of May.

The response to these missions was the equipment of a special mission, in the spring of 1858, to the Khanates of Khiva and Bokhara, under Colonel Ignatieff.

The Supreme-Governor, and the Governor-General of Orenburg, had become convinced of the necessity of sending an agent to Turan before the arrival of the Asiatic envoys at St. Petersburg. Since the year 1842 the Russians had had no relations, hostile or friendly, with the Central Asian Khanates. "The information," says Mr. Zalesoff, as translated by Mr. Robert Michell, in one of his valuable contributions to the history of the relations of Russia with the Khanates of Central Asia, " which had been acquired through previous missions, was out of date, and in respect to the topography of the country, it bore only on localities in proximity with Bokhara and Khiva, without any reference whatever to the main artery of Central Asia—the Oxus—which, as regards commercial as well as political relations, is of such immense importance. Moreover, while in 1853 we had brought our line of forts down to the Jaxartes, and so placed ourselves in immediate relations with the Khanate of Khiva, we not only wanted correct information concerning the condition of the Central Asian states, their mutual relations, the territories of Bokhara, and other territories along the Oxus ; we had, moreover, unfortunately only a very vague idea of the localities on this (the Russian) side of the Jaxartes. These circumstances were sufficient of themselves to call our attention to the study of the country on our borders, and to the conterminous portion of Central Asia. In addition to this, the hampering of our trade by the Asiatics with enormous duties, the solution of the question as to the possibility of conveying our merchandise by river (Oxus), the detention of captives, &c., involuntarily compelled us to make one more effort to persuade the rulers of Turan to be more reasonable in their behaviour towards Russia, and to adopt conduct which would be more advantageous to themselves. Entertaining these ideas, our Government determined all the sooner to follow them up, since it had received the verbal assurance of the Khivan envoy, and that of the Ameer, of their wish to see an agent of ours in their respective Khanates."

On the receipt of imperial commands relative to the despatch of an agent to the Khanates, preparations were at once commenced at Orenburg for the equipment of a mission. The road selected for the march of the mission was the one which passes by the former site of Fort Emba, along the west coast of the Aral, and so on to Khiva and Bokhara, the return being again through Khiva. A detachment of Cossacks was ordered to escort the mission along the shores of the Aral, while, for the better examination of the course of the Oxus, a portion of the Aral flotilla was placed at the orders of the agent.

At that time the steppe under the Orenburg jurisdiction, and more particularly the western half of it, across which the path of the mission lay, was in a state of agitation. For two consecutive years Russian detachments had been unceasingly pursuing the band of a notorious Kirghiz batyr, or freebooter, Iset Kutebar; but to no purpose. This son of the steppes, each time that the Russians got upon his track, decamped to the centre of the Ust-Urt, into which, owing to the complete exhaustion of their horses, and to the scarcity of fodder and water, the pursuing detachments could not follow them. This was the condition of affairs even in the year 1858; so that in order to guard the mission against an attack from Kutebar, it was necessary to give it the protection of a convoy. The agent was provided with a guard of honour, consisting of fifty-seven men, who were to attend him in the Khanates. In addition to these the Governor-General of Orenburg, proceeding as far as the Emba with the mission, was to detach seventy-five men from his own convoy, sending them on with the mission as far as the first Khivan settlement. Moreover,

Lieutenant Skriabin, of the Corps of Topographers, under orders to execute a reconnoissance during the summer along the western limits of the Ust-Urt, was directed to send across the Ust-Urt a flying party of 150 Cossacks to afford assistance, if it should be necessary, to the mission in its progress along the west coast of the Aral.

CHAPTER IX.

IGNATIEFF'S MISSION TO KHIVA AND BOKHARA
(continued).

No expense was spared in the equipment of the embassy. The staff of the mission consisted of the agent, Colonel Ignatieff, the secretary, two interpreters, two officers of the general staff, two officers of the Corps of Topographers, two doctors, one naval officer who was an astronomer, a photographer, a civil official of the Governor-General's staff, and three topographic clerks. There were also an official from the Academy of Sciences, sent for the purpose of studying the Eastern dialects, a priest proceeding to join the Aral flotilla, and a student of the University of St. Petersburg, attached at his own request, and desirous of going as far as Khiva, in order to study the nature of the steppes. The convoy was composed of picked men, consisting of twenty-three mounted Fusiliers, seventeen Orenburg Cossacks, seventeen Ural Cossacks, and nine Cossacks unattached, with an excellent rifled piece of ordnance, and seven officers.

Besides a variety of articles for use, the mission was supplied with astronomical, photographic, and geodesical instruments, and with sketching materials, as well as with the results of steppe surveys, and of surveys made in the Khanates on previous occasions.

For the carriage of two months' supply of provisions and forage, 220 camels were hired at six roubles per month each, and for the transport of the baggage belonging to the members of the mission, 110 camels were engaged, at the rate of fifteen roubles each from Orenburg to Khiva. These were attended by a regular number of servants under a caravan bashi; the full strength further comprising four Kirghiz messengers and two guides.

The mission started to traverse the Barsuk sands and the barren and arid Ust-Urt desert, with twenty-three carriages, ambulance waggons, and carts, and nearly 200 horses, exclusive of the supplementary convoy of seventy-five men from General Katenin's detachment.

The vessels of the Aral flotilla were being prepared for this service simultaneously with the equipment of the mission.

In despatching the agent to the Khanates, the War Ministry directed him to obtain as much information as he possibly could respecting the topography of these little-known countries, as well as the Kirghiz steppes, of which the official survey was to be verified. He was instructed to keep a topographical diary during the journey, to write geographical and statistical descriptions of the countries passed through; to collect information concerning the ancient bed of the Oxus, the Turcomans, their military force and their relations towards their neighbours, the roads passing through the Khanates to neighbouring Asiatic states, the military resources of the Khanates and conterminous countries, and, above all, the course of the River Oxus, of which a careful study was to be made.

Towards the end of April the officers composing the mission assembled at Orenburg, Colonel Ignatieff arriving there on the 1st May (1858). Preparations for their departure were being made night and day. "It is almost impossible," writes Mr. Zalesoff (Mr. Robert Michell's translation), "for those who have served only in the interior of Russia, and who are accustomed only to European modes of conveyance, to realise the great difficulty of equipping troops for the steppes. The equipment and despatch of little more than 100 men demanded a great deal of minute consideration concerning dress, supply, and transport. With all the assistance of the local departments and of various individuals, and after six months' persevering labour, General Katenin could only just arrange for the departure of the mission by the middle of May. The 15th of May opened with a fine spring morning; and at 8 o'clock all the members of the mission were attending prayers on the wide plain beyond the Ural river. The final benediction was pronounced, the command was given, and the mission filed away into the vague distance, ignorant of the fate that awaited it."

The spring of 1858 was exceptionally favourable for movements in the steppe. The fodder under foot was everywhere good, and over the first stages of its march the mission was accompanied by rains and a cool atmosphere.

Carefully considering the eventualities of his position in the Khanates, and bearing in mind the wiliness displayed by Asiatics in negotiation, Colonel Ignatieff wrote as follows to the director of the

Asiatic Department, General Kavalewski, from the bivouac at Bish-Tawak, on the 24th May:—

"While wending my way across the steppe I have been thinking over the business which is before me in Khiva and Bokhara, and have determined to tell you some of the ideas which have occurred to me in trying to reconcile the information on Central Asia obtainable at Orenburg with the instructions which have been given to me. I beg your Excellency will treat these lines as candid gossip, to which you repeatedly challenged me before I left St. Petersburg, and not as the expression of any misgivings.

"Making a sacrifice of myself for the benefit of the service, I am not afraid of my candour.

"When the time comes for negotiating with the Khans, I shall be entirely guided by what, to the best of my judgment, will be most advantageous to us and most compatible with the general views of the Ministry, in the event of any doubts, or of any disaccordance of local circumstances with my instructions; and I have considered it my duty to acquaint you beforehand with my view of the commission entrusted to me by order of His Imperial Majesty, seeing that there is even yet time to send me positive ministerial orders in case it should be found that I am in error.

"It is said in my instructions, that in case the Government of Bokhara consents to all our demands, I am to promise compliance with the requests preferred by the envoy, Mir-Akhur Mulladjan. The first of these requests was that Bokharian merchants should be allowed to visit all towns and fairs, without any exception, within the Russian Empire; and the second, that separate shops should be assigned to Bokharian traders at the Nijni Fair, at a permanent charge, whether they be occupied or not. The Orenburg authorities have endeavoured to convince me that for many years past Bokharians have been in the habit of visiting all the towns and fairs in the Russian Empire, and that, by authority long ago granted, nineteen shops at Nijni Fair were assigned to them on payment in advance of a fixed charge; and, moreover, that the Bokharians, having ceased to pay for these shops in advance, the Court of Management let them to other tradesmen. In November last (1857) they paid into the hands of the Frontier Commission the sum of 810 roubles for nine shops, for the present year, 1858. The Commission forwarded the money to the Military Governor of Nijni Novgorod, and the shops will be at the disposal of the Bokharians. As far as I can make out, from conversations with the Bokharian envoy, the Bokharians desire a certain number of shops to be definitively assigned to them, as in the case of the Chinese. In regard to the privilege which is sought, of trading throughout Russia without hindrance, it seems to me that the Bokharians mean thereby, that they wish to be freed from the obligation of taking out trade certificates, and to replace them by a permanent charge, as has hitherto been done in their case only at Nijni, Irbit, Tiumen, and Korennoi fairs. I do not know whether this interpretation of the Bokharian demand falls in with the views of the Ministry. In order not to promise too much, I shall, in drawing up the 'Obligatory Act' which I have to submit to the Ameer, endeavour to employ the same words as those in which the promises to be made are expressed in my instructions; but I fear that the Bokharians will not appreciate these privileges, and that the Ameer will not consider himself sufficiently compensated for his signature to the Act.

"It is doubtful whether the Khans of Bokhara and Khiva will consent to admit resident Russian commercial agents in their capitals; but it may be that their consent to our demands will be made conditional upon the admission of their own agents to our fairs. Shall I agree to this or not? I imagine that the first would prove of advantage to us; and I not only believe that the 'Act' should include provisions for the residence of Bokharian and Khivan agents in Orenburg, but I intend to hint to the Khans, in the course of negotiation, that in the event of our demands being acceded to, there shall be reciprocity in the matter of the agencies; and I shall endeavour to prove to them all they might gain through permanent agencies at Orenburg.

"As the promises which we shall make in return for what we demand from the Rulers of Bokhara and Khiva will in reality be insignificant, and will mainly consist of loud and empty phrases,* would it not be better to convince the Khans of the necessity of accepting and signing the terms proposed to them by means of a threat, to the effect that in case of refusal we shall withhold all the privileges hitherto extended to Asiatics in matters of trade, telling them at the same time that we can do very well without Asiatic merchandise? Will the

* These remarkable words are literally translated from the Russian original.

Ministry approve of my conduct, and will it support my threats in case of need? At all events I intend, as a last resource, to try my method of persuasion.

"I am also instructed to give the Ameer no positive answer if he should ask our assistance in his war with Kokand, and to be circumspect in my dealings with envoys, and with others from Tashkend. According to the latest intelligence, the Kokandians continue to be secretly and openly hostile to us. It appears to me that the dignity of Russia requires that we should treat the Kokandians as people who have merited chastisement, and that we should not only avoid all dealings with them, but also speak of them in Bokhara, where their acts of hostility against us are well-known, as robbers, with whom it is not worth our while to transact any business, and upon whom we mean to inflict punishment at the first opportunity.

"It would hardly be advantageous to us to refuse aid to the Ameer of Bokhara in his war with Kokand, in the event of his applying to us for it, and thereby to lose the opportunity of connecting the Syr-Daria (Jaxartes) lines by occupying Turkestan and Tashkend.

"Even if the Khanate of Bokhara were to gain strength at the expense of Kokand, it could not become formidable to us, owing to the effeminate character of its people, and also because it would be difficult for the Ameer—as has been proved on former occasions—to keep the conquered provinces of Kokand in due subjection. To co-operate, even morally, with the Kokandians against the Bokharians, would be directly in opposition to our interests. A reliance on our aid from this side would make the Ameer more willing to comply with all our demands. While, on the other hand, seeing no direct advantage in an alliance with Russia, the cunning and experienced Ameer would probably treat me in the same manner as he treated our Mission in 1841, which was very badly received, and completely unsuccessful, not only failing to make the Ameer agree to any one of our demands, but being moreover subjected to various indignities.

" In order to induce the Khan of Khiva to permit Russian vessels to ply freely on the Oxus, it will be necessary to promise him some pecuniary advantage. He might be told that the caravans which now proceed by way of Bokhara to Russia bring him no profit, but that the commercial navigation of the Oxus would divert all the traffic through Khiva, and that Russia would consent to a transit duty of two-

and-a-half per cent. on all goods passing up and down the river in vessels through the Khivan dominions, which would plainly tend to increase the Khan's revenues. This rate of duty would not be burdensome to us.

"It will, in any case, be necessary to consent to the imposition of this duty for the first two or three years, after which, on the extension of navigation on the Aral sea and on the river Oxus, it will be easier for us to demand its abolition in respect to cargoes which are not discharged within the Khivan dominions."

From the Bish Tamak bivouac Colonel Ignatieff despatched a special messenger to Captain Butakoff, commanding the Aral flotilla, requesting him to communicate with the Mission on its reaching Chernisheff bay, explaining that "the necessity of clearly indicating the respective operations of the Mission entrusted to me and the Aral flotilla, in their farther progress to the confines of Khiva, and of coming to an understanding concerning the difficulties which the flotilla may encounter upon entering the mouth of the Oxus, make it imperative that we should meet as speedily as possible before determining our future course of action."

On 31st May the Mission safely reached the Emba, travelling 438 verts (292 miles) in seventeen days, with its enormous transport.

The marauding excursions of the robber Iset Kutebar have already been referred to. After the employment of every means for the pacification of the nomads, the Governor-General of Orenburg thought proper to proclaim an amnesty to the rebel Kirghizes, and towards that end entered indirectly into communication with Iset himself, in order to induce him to present himself with a petition for pardon. In spite of the strong persuasions of those who acted on behalf of the Governor-General, Iset—advised, it was said, by his mother—at first positively declined to have any dealings with the authorities at Orenburg, and was preparing to migrate to the Ust-Urt, when he suddenly heard of the advance of the Mission under the Emperor's Aide-de-camp, and changed his mind. He resolved, before proceeding to an interview with the Governor-General, to give himself up to the Envoy, as one who might be considered in the confidence of His Majesty the Czar. On the 4th of June, Iset, with some of his companions, stood unarmed in the tent of Colonel Ignatieff.

"After the first compliments," wrote the agent, "Iset professed a complete submission to the Government, begging me, as the Envoy of His Imperial Majesty, to assure the Emperor of his submission, and his desire to atone for former misdeeds by zealous and faithful services. He, at the same time, explained that, owing to the dishonest and unscrupulous behaviour of the subordinate and commanding officers hitherto sent into the steppe, from whom he had suffered persecution, he could not treat with them in any way, but had waited for the appearance in the steppe of a man who would personally assure His Imperial Majesty of his obedience, and vouch for his security if he went to present himself to the Governor-General."

Four days after his submission, Iset led the embassy through his aùls, gave trusty guides to conduct the Mission over the Barsuk sands, and made his favourite son accompany the Agent to Khiva, to show the Khivans how thoroughly devoted he was to the Russian Government. Immediately upon reaching the Chegan river, on 7th June, the Agent, in accordance with his previous letter to Captain Butakoff, sent off a topographer, with two guides, to Chernisheff bay, in order to open communications with the flotilla; and, directing the caravan to proceed somewhat more slowly across the sand, he himself emerged upon the shores of the Aral on 12th June, waiting impatiently for the appearance of the vessels. But it was found impossible to remain any longer at Chernisheff bay, owing to the utter absence of fodder and insufficiency of fresh water. The detachment was obliged to resume the march, and to perform a long and tedious night journey to the nearest wells.

The dilatory despatch of various stores from Orenburg had detained Captain Butakoff at Fort No. 1 longer than he had anticipated, so that he was not able to keep his appointment with the Agent at Chernisheff bay. On 14th May the Mission encamped at Cape Bai-Gubet, whence they beheld the black figure of the steamer *Perofski* passing by them without noticing the signals from the shore. On the 19th, however, after many efforts to open communications with Colonel Ignatieff, Captain Butakoff had the satisfaction of meeting the head of the Mission on the barren shores of the Aral.

After the interview with Butakoff, the Agent wrote as follows: "I have shown Captain Butakoff the resolution of the Committee forwarded with your

Excellency's letter of the 15th April, and have advised him not to make the preliminary survey of the Oxus up to Kungrad, which he holds to be necessary. It appears, according to the information received by Captain Butakoff as to the present condition of the mouths of the Oxus, that the Taldyk has become shallow, and that the main body of water flows into the old or eastern channel. The mouth of the Taldyk has been mentioned by Captain Butakoff as the point of rendezvous for the flotilla, which, composed of the steamers *Perofski* and *Obrucheff,* and of the three barges, will assemble there on the 23rd. Taking two of these vessels, laden with presents, Captain Butakoff will proceed to the mouth of the Oxus, and ascend to Kungrad, acting upon instructions contained in a letter which I this day despatched by messenger to the Commandant of Kungrad. I have requested Captain Butakoff to pay no attention to any act of hostility on the part of individual Khivans, or any attempts to stop the steamers; to communicate with me as often as possible; and, in particular, to inform me without delay of any stoppage that may occur; desiring him, moreover, to be at Kungrad by the 25th. In the event of any unforeseen hindrances to the passage of our boats, the presents will be transferred to Khivan barges, in charge of Mojaisky (a naval officer) and Lalatzky (staff officer), with two of our soldiers."

Having determined upon this, merely with the object of effecting a survey of the river, Colonel Ignatieff at the same time resolved to change the route of the Mission itself, which he now directed towards Kungrad instead of Kuna-Urgendj. For the double purpose of acquainting the Khivan authorities with the reason for the entry of the vessels into the Oxus and for the change of route, and of ascertaining the impression produced on the Khivan Government by these proceedings, the Agent sent on ahead a man named Panfiloff, a clerk of the merchant Zaichikoff, in charge of the latter's mercantile venture.

This man, who had before been in Central Asia, is described by the historian of Ignatieff's expedition as "one of those many Russians who are so clever at finding out everything, and whose sound commonsense enables them to emerge from every difficulty."

After arranging accordingly and directing the course of the Mission to Urga, on Aibugir bay, Colonel Ignatieff considered it necessary to furnish the commander of the flotilla with special written instructions, in addition to verbal explanations, from which the following extract may be made, in order to throw more light on the proceedings of the Mission :—

"The preliminary survey of the estuary of the river, of which the necessity is recognised, could be permitted only on the condition of your employing great caution in its performance and of its not entailing any evil consequence on the Mission and on the flotilla in the furtherance of their object—the securing of a free passage up the Oxus."

Parting from the flotilla, and performing two more marches along the west coast of the Aral, the Mission came to a halt at Urga, by Aibugir lake, an arm of the sea now completely choked with reeds.

During this movement, the reconnoitring detachment under Lieutenant Skriabin traversed the Ust-Urt and entered into communication with the Mission; but Colonel Ignatieff, having no occasion for its services, directed Lieutenant Skriabin to proceed to fulfil the duties with which he was charged.

On the road to Urga the Mission was met by Kirghiz messengers, who had been sent to Khiva by the Governor-General of Orenburg, with a notification of the despatch of the Mission. These Kirghizes having interviewed the Mehtar and the Khan himself, were the first to inform the Agent that the Khivans were very much alarmed by the Governor-General's progress through the steppe and by the movements of the various detachments, as well as by the numerous escort attending the Mission. They feared that the Russians would form an alliance against them with the Turcomans, and the Kirghizes inhabiting the southern portion of the Khanates, whose chief, Asbergen, was a near relative and confederate of Iset. In apprehension of such an the alliance with the Turcomans, the Khan, through these Kirghiz messengers, requested the Mission to proceed to Kungrad instead of Kunia Urgendj. In this the desire of the Khan thoroughly conformed with the intentions of the Agent himself. The Governor of Kungrad, with a convoy of 100 horsemen, under the command of the Kungrad officials, was instructed to meet the Mission; and the Divan Baba, the brother of the Divan Begi, or secretary and treasurer of the Khan, was appointed as permanent attendant upon it. When within four miles of Urga, the Mission was met by the commanding officers of the Khivan convoy, who secretly endeavoured, in the course of conversation, to ascertain the objects of the Mission and its relation with the Turcomans.

Four days were employed in the tedious passage of the Aibugir in Khivan boats. Eight consecutive hours passed in the reeds during sultry heat, afforded the first experience of the tortures which were subsequently to be endured in the navigation of the Oxus.

The supplementary convoy was sent back to the Uralsk fort from Urga, and here, in view of the impossibility of conducting the heavy transport through a country offering constant impediments, the officers' and other carriages were burned. The four carriages sent back with the supplementary convoy left only two light carts for invalids to follow with the Mission. At this place the number of non-combatants was reduced, the feeble-bodied men were eliminated from the escort, and the complement was filled up with ten Aral Cossacks from the supplementary escort.

Marching from the Aibugir to the place of residence of Iset Kutebar's relative, Asbergen, who appeared before Colonel Ignatieff with offers of submission, the Mission entered Kungrad the next day (28th July). It passed through an immense crowd of people, and, wending its way along dirty streets, reached the Khan's palace, which strongly resembled a prison and which was intended for the accommodation of the Mission. The information received from the Kirghiz messengers concerning the apprehensions at Khiva was found at Kungrad to be correct; and the fear and mistrust which filled the minds of the Khivan officials became evident in their relations with the Mission and in their references to its possible objects. In a cyphered despatch from Kungrad, the Russian Agent reported to the Minister for Foreign Affairs as follows :—

"We arrived safe and well at Kungrad on the 28th. Our reception was good; but our position is becoming embarrassing. The friendly letter sent by General Katenin to the Turcomans has been intercepted by the Khivans, who regard it as evidence of our duplicity." (The letter in question gave intimation of the progress of the Russian Mission.) "Of the four Kirghiz couriers carrying letters, three were seized and conveyed to Khiva; the fourth came to meet me with a complaint. Our detachment and the progress of the Governor-General threw the Khanate into agitation; the militia were called out everywhere. Matters were aggravated by the steamer. I am being hurried to Khiva; but I am endeavouring to gain time. I was first temporising on account of the steamer; now it is with a desire to clear up matters. The steamer attempted a passage up several mouths, causing great alarm by firing guns and by its efforts to ascend the river. From the 22nd up to the 28th it failed in these efforts, so that I was obliged to agree to the persistent demands of the Khivans that the presents should be transferred to Khivan boats. I am loitering to gain time, but I am going forward. In Kungrad I take to Khivan boats."

Everything, indeed, tended to increase the terror of the mistrustful Khivans. The Khivan Government, having received information from the Jaxartes concerning the preparations for the despatch of the flotilla, determined forthwith, at all hazards, to prevent its entry into the Oxus; and the Governor of Kungrad, under the penalty of losing his head, began on the 24th of June to urge Colonel Ignatieff to order the vessels not to enter the river. Having already given instructions for the ascent, the Agent was obliged to make some delay, both in his own movements and in the issue of instructions to stop the flotilla, which naturally did not serve to pacify the Khivans. Failing to find a passage from the 22nd to the 28th of June, Captain Butakoff, by his persevering efforts, necessarily attracted the attention of the Khivan officials, who had stringent orders from the Khan to stop him; and he at last drove them to despair when, on the 29th of June, the *Perofski*, with a barge, discovering a new arm of the Oxus, the Ulkun-Daria, passed the bar and steamed up towards Kungrad. The barge, saluting Captain Butakoff's cutter with a fire from its guns, convinced the Khivans of the sinister object of the Russian enterprise.

Considering the movements of the Russian troops on the Ust-Urt; the visit of the Governor-General to the Jaxartes with an enormous suite, previous to the arrival of the Russian Mission in the Khivan dominions; and the interception of the letters addressed at General Katenin's direction by the Sultan Ruler to the Turcomans, one can comprehend the Khivan apprehensions in regard to the Russian alliance with the Turcomans, Khiva's most determined enemies. In these circumstances, regarded with suspicion and ill-feeling by the authorities at Kungrad, and learning that his letters to Russia were being intercepted on their way, Colonel Ignatieff, in response to the pressing requests made by the Khivan officials in the Khan's name that he should hasten to Khiva, resolved, without waiting longer for Butakoff at Kungrad, to embark in Khivan boats, and proceed to the capital. He considered, too, that he would thus have an opportunity of examining the greater portion of the river's course. The horses belonging to the Russians, with a portion of the escort, were, at the request of the Khivans, conducted to Khiva by land on the right bank of the river, under the charge of Captain Borodin, of the Ural Cossacks, and accompanied by a telegraphist named Zelenin.

At the same time the Agent despatched Lieutenant Mojaiski to Captain Butakoff, "under the plausible pretext of obtaining the presents from the steamer, but really with the object of enabling that officer to examine the Taldyk arm, of entering into communication with the flotilla, of ascertaining what had happened to it, and of acquainting Captain Butakoff with the state of affairs." Mojaiski descended the Taldyk, but passing into another arm was obliged to return to Kungrad, where he found the Russian steamers at anchor.

The Mission, accompanied by the Divan-Baba, then proceeded up the Oxus, in Khivan boats, on the 1st of July, both banks of the river being extensively flooded. The Mission suffered much during this passage, in a temperature of 36° Reaumur (113° Fahrenheit), without a breath of wind, almost motionless, under a broiling sun by day, and in dense vapours. They were at night towed along, according to one of the officers with Colonel Ignatieff, " at the rate of speed of the crayfish."

The following extract is from a private letter sent home by this officer:—

" We were at first interested in the novelty of proceeding up the river in Khivan boats. As the Oxus is entirely unknown, we prepared ourselves, as it were, for discoveries in the new world; but, alas! our illusions were soon dispelled. The boats, four persons in each, followed one another at the rate of from two to three versts an hour. Under any circumstances to be rowed is not a lively mode of navigation, but with the Khivan boatmen it is simply torture. The Khivans are terribly afraid of the sail, so when our men stretched out the canvas the Khivans were impatient until what they call the *shaitan,* or devil, was taken down. Our passage from Kungrad to Urgendj lay past the towns of Hodjeili and Kipchak, up the main stream, along narrow channels forced by the water through dense masses of reeds, and by the artificial drains which, owing to a superabundance of water, had been converted into large canals. This year the river is exceedingly full, and the natives say they have not had such extensive floods for a very long time. In many places the inundation spreads over some four or five versts of country, submerging gardens and habitations. We passed most of the night in the reeds, which are taller than a man. Our sufferings were intolerable. During the day we lay almost motionless, stripped to our underclothing, the perspiration streaming from us. At sunset myriads of gnats came forth, and so disfigured our bodies and our faces during the night, stinging us through linen vestments and coats, that we were not to be recognised. Under the canvas stretchers it was suffocating, yet it was impossible to expose one's self. So it was by day. Even the boatmen, who were used to all this, sheltered themselves under awnings. We crossed from one side of the river to the other at haphazard; the Khivans giving the boats up to the mercy of the stream, and not caring where they might be stranded. We got into two dreadful whirlpools, and if we did not sink to the bottom of the Oxus, it was only because it was not God's will that we should do so. Yet the river is undoubtedly grand, being nearly at all points from 4,000 to 6,000 fathoms wide."

When the Russian vessels had forced their way to Kungrad, the Mission was being drawn up the stream, and the Agent was in utter ignorance of the proceedings of the flotilla, the Khivans in his company being all the while fully cognizant of them, as they were informed of events at each point of communication with the shores. It was only on the 15th of July, when Urgendj was being approached, that letters were received by Colonel Ignatieff, through Iset's son and a Khivan courier, from Captain Butakoff, at Kungrad, and from the officers accompanying the horses. These letters fully disclosed the evil designs of the Governor of Kungrad, Esaùl-Bashi, under whose directions all letters were taken from the Russian messengers and read. It was due to the dignity of the Russian Agent that such conduct should not be overlooked, and Colonel Ignatieff accordingly expressed his dissatisfaction to the Khivans around him, with regard to the conduct of Esaùl-Bashi, the Governor of Kungrad. Colonel Ignatieff reported home as follows :—

"Deeming it advisable to give some of the Khivans a lesson, and to show them that I was not inclined to suffer such indignities, I stopped the boats before reaching Urgendj, summoned the Divan-Baba, and explaining to him the impropriety and unpardonable nature of his countrymen's proceedings, declared that if my dissatisfaction with the Esaùl-Bashi were not immediately reported to the Khan, coupled with a request that arrangements be instantly made to facilitate the advance of the horses and half of the escort to Khiva, I should not only discontinue my ascent of the river, but should forthwith return to Kungrad. The Divan-Baba entered with excuses, begging me at any rate to proceed as far as the Urgendj wharf. He said that my return to Kungrad would bring him to the scaffold. He despatched a report to the Khivans, and guaranteed the fulfilment of all my demands."

"While yet on the Ust-Urt," Colonel Ignatieff wrote, "I discussed with Captain Butakoff the question of navigating the Oxus this year, and that officer explained to me that the steamer *Obruchef* was to be left out of all consideration, because she could go to sea only in fair weather, and was wholly incapable of making way against the current of so wide and rapid a river as the Oxus. He furthur said that it was doubtful whether the steamer *Perofski* could ascend the river any distance, for, should the water fall, she might be shut in there for the winter. Captain Butakoff thought it undesirable to run the risk of wintering with the flotilla in that river. Taking the above into consideration, and seeing no use for a steamer in the river with an insufficient supply of fuel, and not feeling authorised to take upon myself the responsibility in opposition to the opinion of the Commander of the flotilla, of incurring the danger to which the *Perofski*, with a barge, might be exposed at Kungrad, and in steaming up to Chardjui and to Balkh late in the autumn, I concurred in Captain Butakoff's suggestion. I was the more inclined to do so because it was not to be expected that the negotiations in Khiva would be concluded in less than a month—not, that is to say, before the end of August. It was, moreover, ascertained that the autumnal rise of water is neither great nor prolonged, and the Commander of the flotilla considered that the navigation of the Aral after the 1st October would be attended with extreme danger. . . . I thought it premature to send the steamer back to the Jaxartes, for the presence of our vessels in the estuary of the Oxus might be a great advantage should we be unable to pass straight on to Bokhara. Subsequently, on the 2nd of August, I received a communication from Captain Butakoff to the effect that, although by the 'arrival of the second barge at Kungrad he was provided with a sufficient store of anthracite to ascend even beyond Chardjui, he still deemed it more prudent to return to the mouth of the river, fearing lest, during the continuance of the negotiations at Khiva, the water, which had already fallen two inches, should become so low as to render it extremely difficult for the vessels to leave the Oxus."

On the 17th of July the mission proceeded up the stream, and passing through several canals, entered the Polovan-Ata, and on the 18th approached the suburban palace allotted to them as their residence during their stay in Khiva. Here they remained eight days, "revelling in fruit and Khivan sweetmeats," before their horses arrived. At length the 28th July was appointed for presentation to the Khan, and at 5 p.m. the Mission was received.

The Russians found themselves in Khiva under circumstances unfavourable to negotiation. The suspicions of the Khivans had been aroused by the military evolutions in the steppes, as well as by the operations of the flotilla; and the Khan's suspicions increased to such a degree that he prohibited all communication with the Mission during the first period of their stay in Khiva, under a penalty of death; caused the Agent's couriers to be seized, lodged them in prison, took all letters, and came almost to the conclusion that Colonel Ignatieff intended to deal by him as the Turcoman Envoy had dealt with Kullu-Murad; in other words, to kill him at the audience.

The position of the officers of the Russian Mission had become exceedingly embarrassing, when intelligence was received in Khiva concerning the appearance of the third Russian vessel (Kolokoltsoff's) in the river; and the Khan sent an officer to ask Colonel Ignatieff "whether he was to be considered as a peaceful Envoy, coming with friendly intentions, or whether he brought war?" The answer given to the Khan, that the third vessel had come with letters, in consequence of the non-receipt in Russia of intelligence from the Mission; a firm protest on the part of the Agent himself against the arrest of his couriers; and the despatch of an officer (Galkin) on the 26th of July to the steamer to fetch the post, at last pacified Said Mahomed, who allowed the steamer to anchor in the Ulkun Daria, and became generally more courteous in his behaviour towards the Russians. The Khan's request that the Envoy should be presented to him without his sword was not consented to; and not only the Agent himself, but all his suite, constantly paraded the town with their side-arms, and in their European dress; a most unusual sight in the Khanates of Central Asia. The Khan's suspicions were not, however, entirely lulled; and he informed the Agent that he would negotiate with him personally, while requesting him, out of regard for his ambassadorial dignity, to let the Secretary and the dragoman of the Mission see the ministers.

On the 2nd of August the Agent informed the Khan Russia's demands, and then commenced " the interminable Asiatic negotiations." On the same day the

Agent despatched a special Kirghiz courier to the Vizier of Bokhara, to announce the arrival of the Mission. On 15th of August, the Kush Begi, in the name of the Khan, invited the members of the Mission to a drive, at the end of which a conference was held by them with five of the ministers. The Khivans were afraid of giving offence to Russia by refusing to agree to the Russian proposals, yet they also feared from Bokhara the consequences of acceeding to them—more especially as regarded the navigation of the Oxus, since the Ameer of Bokhara had, through his Envoys, repeatedly urged the Khan not to allow Russian vessels, under any pretext, to ascend the river. Nevertheless, the Khivans, "moved by impotent malice towards the Ameer," strove all the while to set the Agent's mind against him, and to persuade him not to go to Bokhara.

While agreeing to all propositions with respect to abstention from brigandage, protection to caravans, &c., the Khivans refused point-blank to accept a clause relative to the navigation of the Oxus.

The Khivan traders were equally opposed to this clause, being fully assured that the transport of merchandise in vessels would throw the whole trade into Russian hands. This idea frightened them very much, and "the most convincing arguments of the Agent" failed to assure them.

The negotiations were protracted; and it seemed that Colonel Ignatieff's persistent demands, even including the one referring to the navigation of the Oxus, were likely to be favourably accepted, when suddenly a fresh report from the Governor of Kungrad dashed all the expectations of the Mission, and put an end to the negotiations.

On 21st August a communication was received in Khiva to the effect that boats were being sent from the steamer *Perofski* to execute surveys and take soundings, and that a Persian captive, escaping from Kungrad, had taken refuge on board a Russian boat, whose surrender the Khivan officers had failed to obtain at the hands of the Russian commander. The Khan assembled a Council, at which it was decided positively to prohibit the entry of the Russian vessels into the river. It was feared that, after exploring the country, the Russians might suddenly take possession of the Khanate, and that if they were allowed to carry away captives with impunity Khiva would be ruined. It was, at the same time, thought that the Russians might be moved to such a proceeding by their friendship with Persia, which, in the opinion of the Khivans, went so far that in Persia " money was being coined in the name of the Emperor, and the Shah was surrounded by a Russian force instead of his own."

"If," writes Mr. Zalesoff, "one reflects how valuable the Persian slaves were to the idling Khivans, the ruin which threatened the latter on the liberation of these slaves—the only labourers in the Khanate—will then become apparent. Acting upon a resolution come to in Council, the Khan demanded (but in vain) the surrender of the Persian fugitive slave, and the cessation of the taking of soundings; to which the Agent replied that he had received no report from the Commander of the steamer, and promised to despatch a letter with the sick officers who were about to take their departure.

At the same time Colonel Ignatieff received information to the effect that Mr. Galkin, whom he had previously sent to the flotilla, had found himself obliged to quarrel with the Khivan who accompanied him, on account of the above-mentioned Persian slave, and was therefore compelled to remain on board the steamer.

Ignatieff did not succeed in the main object of his mission. He could not, that is to say, gain permission to navigate the Oxus. But he afterwards obtained this right from the Emir of Bokhara, whom he visited in his capital.

The following extract from a private letter from one of the officers of the Mission conveys an idea of their mode of life in Bokhara :—

" We are in Bokhara, the great seat of wisdom in Central Asia. What can I tell you of this capital, with its sixty or seventy thousand inhabitants? Read the descriptions of it by Meyendorf, Burnes, and Khanikof, written some scores of years ago, and you will form a correct idea of the place. Everywhere clay and dirt, everything stagnant, and so, most probably, things will remain until some power shakes up these Bokharians. The Ameer is a despot in the fullest sense of the word; nobody's life is valued by him at a single farthing. The merchants trading with Russia do not dare even to imagine that any place is better to live in than Bokhara, and, when appearing before the Ameer, they tell him that Moscow, St. Petersburg, or London are not fit to be the soles of Bokhara's boots; that there is nowhere to be found such equity, trade, or wealth as in their own country; and as for cultivation of the mind, I need not say a word. In short, at every step you find self-infatuation, against which diplomacy is utterly powerless, and if the Ameer does indeed make any concessions, believe me, it will only be matter of form. There is a host of so-called learned men (in the Mussulman sense) here; Mullahs and Medressehs are to be seen everywhere, and this is, perhaps, the chief reason of the complete stagnation in the life of the people. What am I to tell you of our situation? They give us food and drink, and we walk about the town in our own costumes, yet, while we are not unfrequently called dogs by the boys in the streets, we are comparatively better off than was Butenef's Mission. The other day the Ameer diverted us with his troop of eight musicians and with several actors, who performed some of the impossible feats which are to be held in our Easter holiday barns. It is said that the principal performer is a fugitive Tartar from Kazan, that he had the felicity to make his first performance before the Ameer, and that, although he was rewarded for it with seventy-five blows with a stick on the soles of his feet, he was nevertheless attached to the Court. The servants of the Governor-General of Bokhara committed themselves in some way or other, and they all had their throats cut; the Governor-General himself was deprived of all his property, which was sold by auction; he himself was treated to forty blows with a stick and put into prison. In all probability his head will be shortly chopped off. This is the kind of justice which is administered here. How can one discuss here on international law, on the power and greatness of Russia, on the development of trade? To begin with, everything must be done here by means of sheer force, and we do not yet wield that; with simple phrases we shall not get very far. . . . Colonel Ignatieff is cheerful and contented; he has obtained all he wanted from the Ameer, and, perhaps, more than he expected. The rest is the business of the Government."

Colonel Ignatieff started, like Bekovitch, in the hot weather, and came back, like Perofski, in the cold. He went through many hardships, encountered many dangers, reached both the distant points for which he had started, and, after a narrow escape of being frozen to death, returned in safety to Orenburg.

"December," says the official narrative, "set in with a terrible snow-storm. The snow-fall became heavy, and the north wind swept over the steppe with all its fury. Colonel Ignatieff was dragging slowly

P

along towards Uralsk Fort with a couple of camels, and his guides informed him one night that they had lost the track, and had strayed to some inlet of the Aral sea; telling him that *shaitan* himself could not find any road in such weather, they left him and disappeared in the snowy maze. The storm became more and more severe, and the cold increased to 20° Reaumur (13° below zero Fahrenheit), with a piercing wind. The Agent's servants were freezing. They moaned in their distress, but there was no means of rendering assistance to them. Towards the evening the cold was still greater. Colonel Ignatieff and the officers with him perceived with terror that the frost was seizing upon them. After fulfilling with success an important commission, after suffering every kind of hardship and privation, they were about to freeze to death in the steppe, to perish at the very threshold of their home, without being able to make an effort to save themselves." It must have been a prayer uttered somewhere for them that in the end saved them; for the guides, remembering them, returned, and with fresh camels. The servants rubbed their frozen faces and hands with snow, while the Agent and his companion jostled each other all night to keep up the circulation. We mention this in order to show what travelling or campaigning in Asia involves, and what stamina, manhood, and health are necessary for service in the steppes. The further progress of the agent, as well as the march of the men behind him, were performed under still more trying circumstances on account of the great depth of snow. The storm pursued them all the way to Orenburg, where the Agent arrived on the night of the fourth of December, the convoy of the Mission marching in at the beginning of February. The journey was begun in a temperature of 30 or 35° R. of heat, and was ended in 35° R. of frost, with constant snow-drifts.

Ignatieff's mission might also be regarded as a military reconnoissance. He made the expedition under conditions which were in many respects new; and the information he brought back as to routes, distances, state of the country, disposition of the tribes, and so on, must have been of great service to General Kauffman when the time came for that Commander to organize the expedition which ended in the subjection of Khiva and its virtual annexation to the Russian dominions.

CHAPTER X.

KAUFFMANN'S EXPEDITION TO KHIVA.

WHEN the expedition of Prince Bekovitch Tcherkaski was despatched to Khiva by Peter the Great; when Orloff, at the orders of the Emperor Paul, marched towards Khiva, with intentions to continue his course through Bokhara to India; when Mouravieff was sent on a mission to Khiva under the Emperor Alexander I. in 1822—the ultimate and avowed object was in each case either to reach or, as Mouravieff put it, to "shake" India. Even in 1839, when General Perofski undertook operations against Khiva, the object of the invasion, as afterwards set forth by its appointed historian, was to weaken the influence and counteract the designs of the East India Company. Five years afterwards, when in 1844 the Emperor Nicholas was endeavouring in London to establish a complete understanding between Russia and England, the importance to England that Khiva, Bokhara and Kokhand should be allowed to retain their independence was fully recognized on the part of Czar. But when, a dozen years ago, the time, not merely for attacking Khiva, but for taking it, had arrived, the new expedition possessed, we were assured, no significance whatever in connection with India!

As, however, Russia's unsuccessful expeditions against Khiva have been related at length, it may be as well to complete the history by giving a brief account of the expedition which in the year 1873 was attended with perfect success. This account will be borrowed in much abridged form from the narrative published by Lieutenant Stumm, who accompanied one of the columns of the expeditionary force as Prussian Commissioner.*

In the year 1872 the Russian Government determined to send another expedition to Khiva; and the question as to the best mode of conducting it occupied the attention of both Adjutant-General von Kauffmann and Adjutant-General Krijanoffsky. The reasons for this step, as officially proclaimed, were

* " Russia's Advance Eastward." Containing the despatches (translated) of the German Military Commissioner, Hugo Stumm, and other information on the subject.—By C. E. H. Vincent.

the acts of hostility committed by the Khan upon the subjects of Russia, which called for punishment on the part of the Czar. In 1871, Colonel Markosoff of the Krasnovodsk detachment had set out with a force in the view of opening up a route to Khiva. On the way he had been attacked by 500 Khivan horsemen, who captured some 150 of his camels at a point where the sandy nature of the ground made it impossible for the Russian cavalry to fight with any effect. Soon afterwards, at the persuasion of the Khan, a body of about 300 Tekkes endeavoured to take the rest of the camels and thus oblige the Russians to retreat. An engagement took place in which the enemy, who took to flight, lost 23 men and the Russians two. Written apologies were soon afterwards brought to the expedition from the Khan himself, who pleaded that the Russian troops had been mistaken for Persians. The professions of goodwill made by the Khivan monarch had, however, no effect on the Russian Government, which was informed of all that had occurred. The Khan undoubtedly possessed great influence over the surrounding nations, and the roving tribes of the steppes; and this influence was always exerted against the interests of Russia. Russian authorities agreed in regarding Khiva as the source of the hostility which had so long hindered the execution of their eastern projects.

But the Khan of Khiva was most anxious to convince Russia of his friendly disposition; and he accordingly despatched an embassy to the Emperor bearing a letter in which he declared that in spite of appearances to the contrary he had always been actuated towards Russia by feelings of friendship and love; offering to give up the Russian prisoners in his power if a treaty were signed between the two Powers that each should be content with its existing frontiers. "But if," continued the Khan, "you make these captives a pretext for hostilities against us in order to extend your dominion, a decree will descend from Providence whose purposes we cannot alter."

No attention, however, was paid to the Khan's assurances; and the Khivan envoys were told by the Russian officials who received them that they could not have access to the Emperor until all the Russian captives in Khivan territory had been released, and the Khan had satisfactorily explained in writing his insolent treatment of the two friendly Missions which had been despatched by General

Kauffmann. The Khan, on learning this decision, replied that he could say nothing further before receiving an answer to the questions he had put in his communication to the Emperor. Consequently negotiations fell through.

The Khan now sought in various quarters protection against Russia, who alarmed him from time to time by sending reconnoitring parties towards his dominions. He despatched ambassadors to England, India, and Turkey, praying assistance in case of need. "The matter," says Lieut. Stumm, "was one in which England could hardly act in total disregard of Russia; and in the end an agreement was come to between the two great Powers by which Russia recognised the right of the Ameer of Cabul to the provinces between the Hindu-Kush and the Oxus, known as Afghan Turkestan (on which Russia's feudatory, the Khan of Bokhara, had claims), and on the other hand was allowed free action by England as far as the Afghan border."

Meanwhile the Khan gave "repeated indications of his ill-will towards the Emperor;" and early in 1872 an expedition to Khiva was, as before mentioned, firmly resolved upon. Before the necessary preparations were commenced, Colonel Markosoff, was instructed to make reconnoissances towards the Khanate; and these were not completed until the end of the year. Then a conference of high officials was held at St. Petersburg to decide as to the best means of conducting operations. It was determined that forces should start from three points: the Caucasus, Orenburg, and Turkestan. Preparations were now at once set on foot, to be completed by March, 1873. The mode of operation decided upon was as follows :—

" The proposed attack to be made from two sides, from the east by the forces from the Turkestan district, and from the west by those from the Orenburg and Caucasus districts together. The destination of the expedition to be the capital of the Khanate; the punishment of which, and the dispersion of the Khivan troops, to be the first care of the Russians.

" The column from Tashkend to be commanded by Adjutant-General von Kauffmann, commanding the Turkestan district, and to be made up of eleven companies of infantry, 200 sappers, 550 Cossacks, 14 guns and a rocket detachment. The column to proceed by way of Djisak, on the road running along the Bokharian frontier to Temer-koudour, Tamol, and Elden-Ata, to join another column from the Turkestan district, consisting of nine companies of infantry, 150 Cossacks, a rocket detachment, and a detachment of mountain artillery, somewhere near Daou-Kara, or Min-Boulak, whichever may be most convenient. The entire strength of the united Turkestan columns will then amount to 20 companies, each about 140 strong, with 12 to 14 non-commissioned officers, and 11 non-combatants; or 2,800 infantry, 700 Cossacks, and 18 guns. The whole force then to proceed directly towards Khiva, crossing the Amu-Daria above Min Boulak, where it will join the columns from Orenburg and the Caucasus, who ought by that time (beginning of May) to reach the left bank of the Amu-Daria. Adjutant-General von Kauffmann will then take the supreme command.

"The Orenburg column, made up of companies of infantry (five of the 2nd Orenburg line battalion, and four of the 1st), 600 Orenburg and 300 Ural Cossacks, six guns of Cossack Horse Artillery, six rocket parties, and six mortars, to concentrate at a spot on the Emba under Lieut.-General Vereffkin. Then to march by way of Karatamak along the western coast of the Aral to Kasarm and Ourg, where it will join the column from the Caucasus.

General Verffkin then taking the command, will, if possible, aid the Turkestan column in crossing the Oxus."

Much activity was displayed in getting everything ready for the various columns. Great difficulties were experienced by some of the contingents on the march to their respective rendezvous whence the columns were to start. Thus the 4th Turkestan Rifle Battalion, stationed at Orenburg when orders arrived for it to form part of the Tashkend column at Kazalinsk, was severely tried on its way to the place of assembly; although nothing had been omitted which could facilitate the march. Well provided with sledges, the first detachment set out on the 1st of February, followed by the other three on the 3rd, 5th, and 7th respectively. The daily stage was 40 miles, and at each station a relay of horses was in readiness. After passing Orsk, however, the men proceeded on foot, because of the excessive cold, which on horseback was unbearable; and for three or four days violent storms accompanied them. They showed great perseverance throughout the trying time, and at length, on the 2nd of March, reached Kazalinsk, with only three cases of sickness, and after having travelled a distance of 670 miles across the steppes in the depth of winter—a feat which, according to a writer on the subject, " proves that Russian soldiers may overcome the utmost difficulties, and surmount every possible impediment."

The constituent parts of the Orenburg column, too, were put to rather a severe test in their march to the appointed place of assembly on the Emba. The first Orenburg line battalion, split up into four companies, proceeded from that town by Iletzk and Ak-Toub, while two sotnias of Cossacks went along the river Xobd; and on March 8th the 2nd Orenburg line battalion, composed of five companies, with four sotnias of Cossacks, left Orsk for the rendezvous.

The daily stage was 27 miles, and at night the men slept in the Kirghiz waggons accompanying the various companies. The temperature was made tolerable by camel dung fires which were kept up throughout the night, and a snow rampart raised round each waggon served as shelter from the piercing winds. Through frosts, snows and gales progress was steadily made, and the whole force had at length arrived safely at the Emba Post, only 45 men being on the sick list.

Information had meanwhile come to hand that Kaphar-Karadjigetoff, a Mangishlak chief, was staying at Khiva as the guest of the Khan, who intended, with his aid, to incite the whole Mangishlak Peninsula against Russia. A short time before Kaphar had assured the Kirghizes that the Russians intended to requisition a large portion of their cattle, and had advised them, as their only means of safety, to emigrate to Khiva, where protection would be found. This counsel had been accompanied with a threat that if they did not act upon it he (the Kaphar) would himself put them to the sword. Terrified, the Kirghizes had hastily commenced to shift with their cattle; and it was now Russia's interest to prevent the exodus and keep the commotion from spreading. Apprised of events, Colonel Lamakin, who was reconnoitring from Fort Alexander, at once made for Bouzach, where the emigrants were said to have halted. At the Kara-Kech Gulf he overtook a number of nomadic tribes with some 10,000 head of cattle on their way to the Ust-Urt. Colonel Lamakin endeavoured to calm their fears and to persuade them to return; but the incredulous Kirghizes suddenly attacked the Cossacks with lance and axe. The latter, however, although greatly inferior in numbers, quickly beat them off, and Colonel Lamakin marched on to Bouzach, where he was joined by a sotnia of cavalry from another regiment. Recent occurrences proved beyond doubt the evil influence exerted by the Khan of Khiva against Russia. In spite of all the measures taken by the local administration, the Kirghizes scarcely ever failed to be affected by the counsels which came from Khiva. The Khan's hostility would doubtless, too, find expression through the plundering hordes from the Ust-Urt, who, in their turn, might, unless great precautions were taken by Russia, stir up the Kirghizes to the Khivan monarch's entire satisfaction. It was resolved, therefore, to station columns of observation between the Caspian and the sea of Aral. A body of 150 Cossacks went from the steppe forts to take up its position with a few companies of infantry, at Sam, the most suitable point for observations and for securing communications between General Vereffkin's column and the army of the Caucasus; one sotnia took up its position at Djebisk to keep off the hordes from the Orsk-Kazalin tract; and one sotnia watched the Mogodjarsk mountains and watercourses.

The conduct of the entire expedition was, as before mentioned, placed in the hands of General Kauffmann, who intended to approach the Khanate on the northern side, taking care in the first place to assure himself as to the tranquillity of Bokhara and other towns whose attitude towards Russia was doubtful. The General attached himself to one of the Turkestan columns, that which was divided into two detachments, the first composed of twelve companies of infantry, fourteen breech-loading guns, two mortars, one rocket, five sotnias of Cossacks, and 6,700 camels; the second of eight companies of infantry, two old ten-pounder cannon, four rifled guns, two mitrailleuses, one rocket division, two sotnias of Cossacks, and 2,800 camels. The other Turkestan column from Tashkend, called the Krasnovdsk, was commanded by Colonel Markosoff. It comprised eight companies of infantry, four sotnias of Cossacks, four 3-pounder guns drawn by horses, four 4-pounders drawn by horses, eight 3-pounders carried by camels, and 3,000 camels. The Orenburg column, under Lieut.-General Vereffkin, was made up of nine companies of infantry, nine sotnias of Ural and Orenburg Cossacks, eight field pieces, four mortars, six rocket detachments, and 500 camels. Finally, the Kinderli column, made up of troops from the Caucasus, commanded by Colonel Lamakin, of which a portion were to be employed in establishing and protecting the communications, consisted of twelve companies of infantry, one sotnia of Cossacks, two sotnias of Tartars, ten guns of various kinds, one rocket division, and 1,300 camels. Thus the total force at the disposal of General Kauffmann was 53 companies of infantry, 25 sotnias of Cossacks, 54 guns, six mortars, two mitrailleuses, five rocket divisions, 19,200 camels.

Upon being informed of all the preparations which had been going on, the Khan of Khiva was in great alarm. He sent his Russian captives to the Kazalinsk column and implored that negotiations might be opened, declaring that he desired to live at peace with Russia. But the commanders of the several columns had been specially instructed on no account to treat with the Khivan monarch. General Vereffkin's column departed from Kungrad and marched in a southerly direction, having the day previous sent on an advance guard under Colonel Leontscheff. At about 4 a.m. a large party of Khivans swept down upon the Colonel's force, but were repulsed with the loss of several killed. General Vereffkin saw nothing of the enemy either on the 24th or 25th of May, and consequently continued his progress southward, leaving

Colonel Lamakin behind to await a detachment of his column which had not yet arrived. When this had come up he was to follow after and overtake the General, so that a united attack might be made on the fortified town of Khodjeili. Every precaution was taken to prevent a surprise, for there could be no doubt that the Khivan cavalry was hovering about ready to snatch the slightest opportunity. At 5 a.m. on the 28th the march was continued towards Kara-Baili. At noon Colonel Leontscheff's troops halted by the side of the stream to breakfast; but before cooking operations were commenced firing was heard about a mile distant. Information soon arrived that an officer of the topographical department, reconnoitring with half-a-dozen Cossacks, had been borne down upon by a very numerous body of the enemy. On reaching the scene of the attack with two sotnias of men, Colonel Leontscheff found that after killing one Cossack, wounding two others, and capturing several horses, the Kirghizes, as they proved to be, had made off. Chase was at once given; but after going some five miles over boggy ground covered with reeds higher than the horsemen's heads, the pursuit was given up, none of the foe having been overtaken. The fruitless result was shortly explained. The fugitives had taken another direction, and next attacked the Russian rear-guard. Colonel Leontscheff again went to give assistance, and this time drove the enemy to bay at a dense forest some distance off. Many of the Kirghizes were killed, and a considerable number of those who escaped lost their horses. A Kirghiz, who had been made prisoner, gave information about the two late attacks. They had been made by the same party of between 400 and 500 men, detached from an army 6,000 strong, sent by the Khan, under the command of his brother to defend Khodjeili. It was made up principally of cavalry, and lay in wait north of the town. The Khan had no knowledge of the columns advancing under Kauffmann and Markosoff; but he was determined in any case to hold out to the last.

A large fortified Khivan camp was now discovered on an arm of the Oxus. It was 875 paces long and 450 broad, surrounded by a deep ditch, with a rampart seven feet high, and generally well-constructed. It had been abandoned on the morning of the same day (26th May), and consequently the enemy could not be far off. In the evening Colonel Lamakin came up with his column, and joined it to that of

General Vereffkin. He had seen nothing of the enemy. Nothing occurred during the night. Early on the 27th the advance was continued. Soon after the start information arrived that a large body of troops, made up of infantry, cavalry, and artillery, awaited the invaders before Khodjeili; that the town itself was fortified; and, in short, that everything was ready to resist the Russian attack.

The order in which the entire column marched was as follows :—The Orenburg force kept on the left, that from the Caucasus on the right of the road, while General Vereffkin, with his staff, led the van. Just behind him were three guns. The camels and baggage were protected by the rear guard, consisting of two companies of infantry, two sotnias of Cossacks, and two field guns. At about 10 o'clock a part of the enemy's forces was espied on the other side of the river, with a number of boats. On the approach of the Russian artillery, a deputation was sent by the Khivans, who offered to surrender with their provisions and boats; but meanwhile they got away with their belongings before the column came within gun-shot.

A quarter of an hour afterwards the enemy was observed proceeding eastward along the Oxus. After moving some distance they stopped, as though awaiting the Russian advance. The Russian cavalry was sent forward at 11 a.m., with two rocket detachments, who fired ten rounds, with some success, on the Khivans, the latter retiring so quickly that the Cossacks could not come to close quarters. Now the column went on without the least show of opposition. But what had already taken place proved that the Khivans, instead of being content to wait until the Russians reached Khiva, and then fight behind entrenchments, had resolved to do all in their power to hinder the march. Consequently, General Vereffkin issued the following order to his officers :—

"The right column will be led by the Caucasus cavalry to the westward of the Khodjeili road, accompanied by two rocket detachments and a sotnia of Ural Cossacks. Col. Lamakin with his staff and the rest of his column will follow. The left wing will be composed of troops commanded by Col. Leontscheff. The head-quarter staff, escorted by the remainder of the Orenburg Cossacks, will march in the centre along the bank of the Amu. The Cossack horse artillery, with four guns, will remain in the immediate vicinity of the head-quarter staff, and behind the same the infantry of the Orenburg column will march to the eastward of the Khodjeili road. The train and the camels will bring up the rear, escorted by two companies of infantry, two sotnias of Cossacks, and two field guns." *

Towards noon the enemy was observed to advance in line; but when about 2,500 yards off, retired slowly towards the town of Khodjeili. A squadron of the Russian right wing charged with success some skirmishers on the left of the Khivan line, and a few shells were fired from the centre battery. These prevented the Khivans from turning face, and they retired to the east and west of the town. At about half-past two the advance was continued, Lamakin and Leontscheff both attacking from their respective positions. In an hour and a half the suburbs were reached, and skirmishing companies sent forward from each of the detachments. A numerous deputation, selected from among the elders of the town, came towards the staff when the Russians were about 500 paces off the gates, saying it was desired to capitulate, and imploring that mercy might be shown. The Khivan troops had evacuated the place, and its inhabitants now came forward and stood bareheaded outside the walls. At the same time, a Kirghiz was

* Translated by C. E. Howard Vincent, in " Russia's Advance Eastward."

given up whom General Kauffmann had sent on a month before with despatches, but who had been made prisoner and maltreated by the Khan.

At 5 o'clock the Russians passed through the town of Khodjeili, and took up a position three-quarters of a mile distant to the south. Representatives from several Kirghiz tribes now came into the camp, complaining of the treatment they had received at the Khan's hands, and asking that they might be looked upon as Russian subjects. Meanwhile, no information had reached General Vereffkin concerning the columns under General Kauffmann and Colonel Markosoff.

On the 30th of May the camp was shifted from Khodjeili to a wood ten miles nearer the Khanate. Early the next morning an attack was made on the outposts by a large body of Yomuds; but they retreated after a few shells had been fired, followed by two sotnias of Cossacks. The latter when they returned, after giving over the pursuit, reported that the Sausan canal, on the way to Mangit, was swollen, and impassable for the infantry. An engineer detachment was thereupon sent forward with casks and other materials for constructing a bridge across. On arriving at the canal, the detachment was fired upon heavily from the underwood on the opposite bank; but the cavalry swam over to the other side, drove the enemy away, and then returned to protect the workmen while engaged in making the bridge, which was soon completed. The entire forces passed over at 8.30 a.m., and encamped on the Oxus. The river here was three-quarters of a mile wide.

According to information brought by Russian spies, the Khivans intended to make a severe attack during the night; but nothing at all occurred. Next morning two shells fired from a great distance by the Khivans fell into the river near the camp. It was now reported that a large body of cavalry and infantry had taken up their position on a hill near the road to Mangit, and purposed to prevent, if possible, any further advance. The town of Mangit, too, was well-fortified and garrisoned.

Careful arrangements were made in view of such an engagement; and the column marched towards Mangit. A little before seven o'clock the enemy was observed at a distance of about three-quarters of a mile southward, occupying a plain, covered with high grass, and mounds near the town. Almost immediately the Khivan cavalry galloped towards the Russians, as if to attack the centre; but soon they altered their course, and went round the flank, intending apparently to commence operations on the train and rear guard. In less than a quarter of an hour they had formed an arc round the column on the south, east, and north-east. A heavy fire was at once begun by four of the centre guns, while the other three were taken to the left flank for the same purpose. Nevertheless, the enemy made repeated charges, and once pressed the cavalry under Leontscheff so hard that not until the men got off their horses and fought on foot could the Khivans be beaten off. Meanwhile the foe had reached the rear guard and attacked it with fury. But the artillery did much execution; and the assailants, seeing that their fellows in front were falling back, retired towards the Mangit heights with considerable losses. A pursuit was now commenced; but with wonderful rapidity the Khivans vanished behind the hills. A quarter of an hour later they reappeared, and began to form for another onslaught. This time they did not come far, for the Russian skirmishers had been sent forward, and these, working in co-operation with the rocket division on the right flank, soon compelled them to retreat towards the town. On their way, however, the Khivans set fire to the village, which was with difficulty extinguished; and at the same time, by some means or other, the steppe behind the Russian forces caught fire, though fortunately, thanks to a favourable wind, the latter conflagration did not approach the Russians. The Russian losses were one captain and eight soldiers killed, ten severely and a large number slightly wounded. The losses on the Khivan side were much greater. After a short rest, Mangit was marched on and occupied by the column without opposition. It was now about three o'clock; and an hour later the column advanced to a position on the Arna canal, three-quarters of a mile southward.

On the 2nd of June, after numerous minor engagements of no importance, the column left Mangit, Lieut.-Col. Skobeleff having been sent on ahead with a body of 200 men to burn Kutebara, a village whose inhabitants had taken a promnient part in recent hostilities as well as in the marauding excursions into Russian territory made some time previously. After continued skirmishing, the Attualick canal was reached towards evening; and here the column passed the night. Next morning the canal was crossed by the wooden bridge stretching over at this point, which the Khivans had not had the foresight to destroy. The enemy now opened a heavy fire from behind, but only succeeded in killing a few camels. Later in the day a Khivan messenger fell into the hands of some Cossack scouts. He was on his way to the enemy's column, and declared, on being brought into the camp, that General Kauffmann had arrived at the right bank of the Oxus, and was trying to get his troops over to the other side of the stream. The Khan, he said, looked for a decisive battle on the morrow, when, under his personal command, all his forces would fight together. The information respecting the Khan proved afterwards to be false; for during the engagement the Khivan monarch kept in his harem.

The camp was pitched on the canal at 6·45 a.m., after every precaution had been taken. The camels and two waggon-trains were formed into a square and protected by a very strong rear guard. Soon the enemy commenced an attack, and at first the Russian position was much endangered; but, thanks chiefly to the infantry, the assailants were kept off. They made, however, repeated onslaughts, and it was not until 11 a.m. that hostilities had ceased. The camp was now moved, and at about four o'clock pitched a few miles south of the village of Udott. The natives here came to the Russians, begging protection against their fellow-countrymen, who, they said, had robbed and maltreated them. They further declared that the Khan's forces amounted to about 7,000 men, whereas the day before the Khivan army had been represented by other informants as 20,000 strong. The Khan, it seemed from these fugitives, had given orders that efforts were above all to be made to destroy the Russian camel train, in order to prevent the invaders from reaching the capital.

A letter was now received from General Kauffmann, addressed to Colonel Markosoff, whose column the messenger bearing it had been unable to find. The General said in the letter that he was on the right bank of the Amu, and was preparing to cross the stream, now much swollen. He hoped to arrive at Khiva on the 5th or 6th of June, and instructed Colonel Markosoff to await his arrival.

During the afternoon of the 6th the Khan, who was in Khiva getting everything ready for the final conflict, sent an envoy to General Vereffkin proposing an armistice. In his letter the Khivan monarch invited the Russian Commander as guest to his capital, declaring that, always cordially friendly disposed towards Russia, he should now take the sincerest pleasure in entertaining personages of such distinction from her dominions. He wanted three or four days' time to make preparations for a befitting reception, and asserted that the men who had recently been attacking the column were Turcoman robbers with whom he was in no way connected; he regarded them, in fact, as his bitterest enemies. General Vereffkin was, however, not to be deceived by such soft words as these. Probably he remembered the end of Prince Bekovitch, who committed the fatal error of accepting an invitation to dine with a previous Khan of Khiva, and thereby lost his head. In any case, General Vereffkin had no inclination to partake of the present monarch's hospitality. He made no reply to the letter.

Next day the Russians had to halt at a canal where the bridge had been burnt by the enemy. Here the camp was pitched, and the construction of another bridge commenced. Colonel Leontscheff was now sent on with all the cavalry to clear the way in front. They swam the river safely, and went forward, returning towards evening with several Turcomans whom, with their horses, they had found unarmed and anxious to give themselves up to the Russians, as they were determined to fight no more for the Khan, who would not, they said, give them the promised pay. Colonel Leontscheff had meanwhile heard it confirmed that the Khan had retired to the capital for the final struggle.

Passing on the evening of June 5th through the abandoned town of Kyat Kungrad, the Russian column arrived towards the close of the next day at Kossk-Kupir. Meanwhile a letter had been received from General Kauffmann, who said that, after a successful engagement with the united Khivan forces and the destruction of a battery on the left bank, his staff and six companies with eight guns had crossed the Oxus, but that the rocket detachment, accompanied by five companies, had gone to the town of Schuraschana. General von Kauffmann knew, he said, that General Vereffkin had taken Khodjeili; but beyond that had no knowledge of his movements.

On June 7th, Vereffkin's column arrived at the gardens of the Khan's summer palace, within three miles of the northern gates of Khiva. Two days were spent here, but in no pleasant manner; for throughout the time the Khivans were incessantly harassing the Russians, and in particular trying to destroy Skobeleff's advance guard, which was at times very hard pressed. The guns on the walls of the town moreover were now used against the invaders. The continued fighting was not without fatiguing effect on the Russian forces; and the anxiety felt by Vereffkin was increased by the ignorance in which he was kept concerning General von Kauffmann. A rumour had, it is true, arrived that the General had for want of provisions been obliged to retire to the Oxus; but this by no means tended to improve the situation.

After careful consideration, General Vereffkin decided to attack the capital without further delay, not waiting for the arrival of the Commander-in-Chief. Accordingly, on the the evening of June the 8th, arrangements were made for a strong reconnoissance on the morrow up to the walls of the town, in order to set batteries which were to commence the bombardment.

At 11 a.m. on the 9th, a party of 400 Cossacks, with a rocket section and eight guns, went forward, accompanied by the staff with four guns. Skobeleff's advance posts were soon reached and sent back to protect the baggage. At 1 o'clock the enemy was observed 160 yards off in the gardens of the suburbs, which were apparently occupied by infantry drawn up in line. When the Russian cavalry and infantry advanced the Khivans retreated amid a number of shells which were fired at them. A quarter of a mile further on a narrow defile, surrounded by houses, canals, and walls, had to be passed; and here, under a fire from the walls of Khiva, the reconnoitring body found itself in considerable danger. Promptly, however, they took shelter behind a wall, and when the guns were brought up a well-directed fire was opened upon the north gate.

The Caucasus and Orenburg infantry were now advancing to the right and left of the road preceded by skirmishers, who maintained a steady fire. In half an hour a good many of the Khivan guns had been silenced, and the Russians marched forward to a brick building in front of the canal bridge leading to the town gate. A well-built barricade here hindered further progress. Meanwhile the Russian battery was shifted to a position on the canal to the left of the road, about 200 yards from the wall, and at once recommenced firing. The Orenburg infantry occupied the left canal, and three companies of the Caucasus infantry the right. As soon as this order had been taken two companies of the Samursk and two of the Abscheronsk regiment, under Major Bourovzoff, charged across the bridge, gained possession of three of the Khivan guns, and took up a position 50 paces from the gate.

At this juncture the city could, according to Lieut. Stumm, who saw all that went on, have been captured. But at the last moment General Vereffkin regretted the independent step he had taken. Previously, not knowing anything certain concerning Kauffmann, the Commander-in-Chief, who, he had reflected might possibly be unable to reach the capital at all, he had thought himself justified in acting directly against Khiva on his own account; more especially as to encamp for any length of time within a few miles of the place, was to remain exposed to the attacks from the .Khivan troops without doing anything towards the reduction of Khiva. This seemed all quite logical; and General Vereffkin was doubtless actuated solely by a desire to do his duty under the circumstances. But when the time came at which he could have made the capital of the Khanate his own, it occurred to him that after all the Commander-in-Chief's orders had been to await his arrival. Perhaps he took into account the probability jealousy on the part of Kauffmann, his superior. However this may be, he now, at the critical point, determined not to strike the decisive blow, but, retracing his steps, to do nothing more than bombard until Kauffmann came up.

To Lieut.-Col. Pajoroff's request for ladders, with which, he said, he could take the town, Vereffkin answered, "You can have none," merely adding, on a protest from the Colonel, "We are going back." Then the four storming companies returned across the bridge, after suffering a loss of four killed and 22 wounded, including a Lieutenant and Major Bourovzoff, wounded by three shots in the arm.

A breaching battery was now employed against the walls; the Khivan shot meanwhile falling thickly amongst the Russians. Shortly after 2 o'clock General Vereffkin was severely wounded in his right eye and had to entrust the command to the chief of his staff, Colonel Sarantschoff. All idea of direct attack had been given up, and the cavalry was ordered to retreat. When the breaching and dismounting batteries had been completed the infantry protecting the work also withdrew, leaving General Skobeleff with a detachment to keep watch on the town.

At 2.30 the staff went back towards the summer palace, arriving there an hour afterwards. The General's wound meanwhile had been attended to, and the formation of a field hospital begun.

At 4 p.m. an envoy from the Khan, whose artillery had ceased firing, came into the camp asking for peace and a cessation of the cannon fire, and saying that within an hour a plenipotentiary would be sent to agree on conditions of surrender. Colonels Lamakin and Sarantschoff, who received the messenger, informed him that the Russians would only cease firing if not another shot came from the walls, if all the armed men left the city, and the Khan formally tendered submission. In this case an armistice would be consented to, and General Kauffmann could on his arrival treat with the Khivans. The envoy was further told that should the Khan recommence firing the bombardment would at once be resumed and the city destroyed.

The Russian artillery accordingly ceased firing at 4.30, but very shortly artillery and small-arm fire reopened from the walls. The Khan now despatched a second messenger declaring that he was not responsible for the proceeding, as the men firing were Yomuds, over whom he had no control. The Khan, who had taken to flight, and left his uncle Emir-Omra to administer affairs, desired peace, and so did the whole city. But the messenger was informed that it was not for the Russians to consider any question as to who was firing. It sufficed that shots were being fired; and the bombardment would immediately be recommenced. At 5 a.m. this was done; and both sides continued operations until 10 o'clock, when the town was burning in several places.

An hour later a letter from General Kauffmann arrived, saying that the Tashkend column was about seven miles from Khiva, on the eastern road, and directing Vereffkin to meet him next morning at a bridge two-and-a-half miles off the east gate, where Emir-Omra, the Khan's uncle, would be, to arrange terms of surrender. The wounded General, however was too unwell to repair to the rendezvous; and Colonels Lamakin and Sarantschoff went in his stead with three companies, two sotnias, and two guns. About 9 a.m. General Kauffmann, the Commander-in-Chief, made his appearance at the place he had appointed.

A long negotiation followed with Emir-Omra, and a treaty of peace drawn up, whose chief conditions, as given by Mr. Howard Vincent in *"Russia's Advance Eastward,"* were as follows:—

"1. That the Khivan territory on the right bank of the Oxus, and the delta of that river up to the Taldik branch, be annexed to Russia.

"2. That from the mouth of that stream the frontier run to the headland and thence, following the southern slopes of the Ust-Urt to the Uzboc or former bed of the Oxus.

"3. That Khiva pay to Russia an indemnity of 2,200,000 silver roubles (about £293,888) towards the expenses of the expedition; but, out of consideration for the poverty of the Khivan treasury, the payment may extend over 20 years, the balance remaining unpaid at the end of each year bearing interest at the rate of 5 per cent. per annum.

"4. That Russians trading with Khiva be exempt from the '*Ziabeta*' or customs dues.

"5. That the Khanate of Khiva consider itself as a dependency of the Russian empire."

The Tashkend column, accompanied by the Khan's uncle and his suite, then marched towards Khiva. The east gate was reached at half-past one; and forthwith General Kauffmann entered the town. At four o'clock Khiva was occupied in every part by

Russian troops. The same evening the Commander-in-Chief visited General Vereffkin in his camp, and inspected the wounded lying there.

Having formally occupied the town, the troops went back to camp. Two or three days afterwards the bazaars were reopened, and business went on as usual; the Russian soldiers spending a short time in sight-seeing and making purchases.

On the 29th of June General Vereffkin, with a number of officers, left Khiva, to return to Russia. Meanwhile they had learned that Colonel Markosoff with the Krasnovodsk column, of which they knew nothing, had been obliged to return by reason of the extraordinary difficulties he had met with on his way.

CHAPTER XI.

THE GOOD AND THE EVIL DONE BY RUSSIA IN CENTRAL ASIA.

THE progress of Russia towards India has by a certain class of politicians and writers in England been regarded with marked approval, while those who watched it with concern have been stigmatized by these approvers both as "alarmists" and as selfish opponents of Russia's civilizing mission. That the type of civilization introduced by Russia into her Central Asian possessions is much higher than that which it displaces can scarcely be denied. But the positive good effected in this way by Russia bears no comparison to the evil she would do could she only carry out the projects harboured by her against our Indian empire. The disorganization of India would be a calamity before which the benefits conferred by Russia on her Central Asian subjects would not deserve to be mentioned.

Russia's first appearance among the populations of Turkestan has been usually signalized by wholesale massacre. But after a time slaves are set free, the cruelties of Eastern punishment are put a stop to, and government, not perhaps of the best kind, but more or less of European pattern, is established.

Mr. Macgahan, in his spirited and picturesque account of the fall of Khiva, has described a massacre of unoffending Turcomans, executed, after the capture of Khiva, upon the Turcomans of the Yomud tribe who were hurrying away with their families, their flocks, and their herds to the desert; and General Skobeleff, in his report of the capture of Geok Tepé describes a worse massacre than even the one which was witnessed by Mr. Macgahan.

"Six sotnias of Cossacks," writes Mr. Macgahan, "were selected to pursue the enemy"—who, be it observed, had not struck one blow at the Russians, but were simply flying from them. "Riding along in front of their line," he continues, "I catch sight of Prince Eugene, who welcomes me to the front with a hearty shake of the hand, and kindly puts me in one of his squadrons as a good point of observation.

The order to advance is passed along the line, and in another moment we are dashing over the desert at a gallop. Ten minutes brings us to the summit of the hill, over which we had seen the fugitives disappear; and we perceive them a mile further on crossing another low ridge. Already the body has ceased to be compact, sheep and goats scatter themselves unheeded in every direction; the ground is strewed with the effects that have been abandoned in the hurried flight, bundles thrown from the backs of camels, carts from which the horses have been cut loose, and crowds of stragglers struggling wearily along, separated from friends and rapidly closed in upon by foes.

"Down a little descent we plunge, our horses sinking to their knees in the yielding sand, and across the plain we sweep like a tornado.

"There are shouts and cries, a scattering discharge of firearms, and our lines are broken by the abandoned carts, and our progress impeded by the cattle and sheep that are running wildly about over the plain. It is a scene of the wildest commotion. I halt a moment to look about me. Here is a Turcoman lying in the sand with a bullet through his head; a little further on a Cossack stretched out on the ground with a horrible sabre cut on his face; then two women, with three or four children, sitting down in the sand, crying and sobbing piteously and begging for their lives; to these I shout *'Aman! Aman!'* ('Peace, Peace,') as I gallop by, to allay their fears.

"A little further on more *arbas,* or carts, carpets and bed coverlets scattered about with sacks full of corn, and huge bags and bundles, cooking utensils and all kinds of household goods.

"Then more women toiling wearily forward, carrying infants and weeping bitterly; and one very fat woman, scarcely able to carry herself, with a child in her arms, which I somehow take for her grandchild. Then camels, sheep, goats, cattle, donkeys, cows, calves and dogs, each, after its fashion, contributing to the wild scene of terror.

"I am at first shocked by the number of Turcomans I see lying motionless. I cannot help thinking that if all these be killed there are no such deadly marks as the Cossacks. After a while, however, the mystery is explained, for I perceive one of the apparently dead Turcomans cautiously lift up his head and a moment after resume his perfectly lifeless position. Many of them are feigning death; and well it is for them the Cossacks have not discovered the trick.

"Delayed somewhat by the contemplation of these scenes I perceive that I am left behind, and again hurry forward. Crossing a little ridge I behold my sotnia galloping along the edge of a narrow marsh and discharging their arms at the Turcomans, who are already on the other side, hurriedly ascending another gentle slope. I follow down to the marsh, passing two or three dead bodies on the way. In the marsh are 20 or 30 women and children up to their necks in water, trying to hide among the weeds and grass, begging for their lives and screaming in the most pitiful manner. The Cossacks have already passed, paying no attention to them. One villanous-looking brute, however, had dropped out of the ranks and levelling his piece as he sat on his horse, deliberately took aim at the screaming group, and before I could stop him pulled the trigger. Fortunately the gun misfired, and before he could renew the cap I rode up and, cutting him across the face with my riding whip, ordered him to his sotnia. He obeyed instantly without a murmur; and shouting '*Aman*' to the poor demented creatures in the water, I followed him.

"A few yards further on there are four Cossacks around a Turcoman. He has already been beaten on his knees, and weapon he has none. To the four sabres that are hacking at him he can offer only the resistance of his arms; but he utters no word of entreaty. It is terrible. Blow after blow they shower down on his head without avail, as though their sabres were tin. Will they never have done! Is there no pith in their arms? At last, after what seems an age to me, he falls prone into the water with a terrible wound in the neck, and the Cossacks gallop on. A moment later I come upon a woman sitting by the side of the water, weeping over the dead body of her husband. Suddenly my horse gives a leap that almost unseats me, my ears are stunned with a sharp, shrieking, rushing noise, and, looking up, I behold a streak of fire darting across the sky which explodes at last among the fugitives. It is only a rocket, but it is followed by another and another; and, mingled with the shrieks of women and children, the hoarse shout of the Cossacks, the bleating of sheep and goats, and the howling of cattle running wildly over the plain, made up a very pandemonium of terror. This lasted a few minutes.

"Then the Turcomans gradually disappeared

over another ridge, some in this direction and some in that, and bugle-call sounds the signal for the reassembling of the troops. As we withdrew I looked in vain for the women and children I had seen in the water. They had all disappeared; and as I saw them nowhere in the vicinity, I am afraid that, frightened by the rockets, they threw themselves into the water and were drowned. It was all the more pitiable," adds Mr. Macgahan, "as, with the exception of the case I have mentioned, there was no violence offered to the women and children. I even saw a young Cossack officer, Baron Krudner, punishing one of his own men with his sword for having tried to kill a woman."

Further on he writes: "I must say, however, that cases of violence towards women were very rare; and although the Russians were fighting barbarians who commit all sorts of atrocities upon their prisoners, which fact might have excused a great deal of cruelty on the part of the soldiers, their conduct was infinitely better than that of European troops in European campaigns."

Mr. Macgahan's verdict as to the general humanity of the Russians does not quite agree with the account he gives of acts of cruelty perpetrated beneath his eyes. But he liked the Russians, he was well received by them, and he was not the man to commit the fault of telling tales out of school. General Skobeleff, in his report of the taking of Geok Tepé, wrote plainly on the subject of a massacre, by which the capture of the place was followed, and, when Mr. Marvin reminded him at St. Petersburg of what he had said about the slaughtering of women, replied with praiseworthy candour that he had set down the exact truth.

"When the dead were counted," he said, "women were found among them. It is my nature to conceal nothing. I therefore wrote, in making the report, 'of both sexes.'" In the report the following passage occurs:—

"The pursuit of the enemy flying from the fortress was continued by the infantry for 10 versts ($6\frac{2}{3}$ miles), and by the cavalry six versts (4 miles) further, and only complete darkness and the thorough dispersion of the enemy caused the chase to be abandoned, and the troops to return to camp. In this pursuit by the dragoons and Cossacks, supported by a division of mountain horse artillery, the killed of both sexes amounted to 8,000 persons .... The enemy's losses were enormous. After the capture of the fortress 6,500 bodies were buried inside it. During the pursuit 8,000 were killed."—"General Skobeleff's Report of the Siege and Assault of Dengeel Tepé (Geok Tepé)"—*Voenni Sbornik,* April 1881, quoted by Mr. Marvin, in his *"Russian Advance Towards India."* General Grodekoff said to Mr. Marvin on this subject: "Many women were killed. The troops cut down everybody. Skobeleff gave orders to his own division to spare the women and children, and none were killed before his eye; but the other divisions spared none. The troops used their sabres like a machine, and mowed down all they met."

As to the good done by Russia in Central Asia, "the Persian and other slaves," writes Mr. Macgahan, "hailed with delight the approach of the Russians; for the emancipation of the slaves has always followed the occupation of any place in Central Asia by the Russians."

According, however, to a Russian General who had had thirty years' experience in Central Asia, the alleged man-stealing on the part of the Turcoman tribes was either an invention, or, at the very least, a gross exaggeration. The real marauders and man-stealers were, he said, the Russians themselves; and he distinctly charges the Cossacks quartered in the territory, governed by Prince Gortschakoff (1854) with provoking the peaceful Kirghizes to rebellion and with capturing Kirghiz children to sell them into slavery.

Here, again, is evidence in favour of the Russians by a truthful writer, Arminius Vambéry; who, apparently because he is our friend, is looked upon as their enemy. Readers of Vambéry will not forget the ghastly account he gives of the open pit kept by the Emir of Bokhun for the reception of his enemies; who were cast into it alive, to be tortured and devoured by swarms of vermin generated from the putrefying carcases of sheep and of other prisoners. "The moment," writes Vambéry, in his "*History of Bokhara*," " that the Russian flag was hoisted on the citadel of Samarkand, the ancient and distant country of Asia entered on the path of the modern world and of modern ideas. Towns and countries, hitherto unknown to the denizens of the western world, have been thrown open, and places where the European traveller could only venture in disguise and at the peril of his life, are now not only free and safe, but actually governed and administered by Christians. Churches and clubs have been opened at Tashkend, Khodjend, and Samarcand; in the first-named city there is even a newspaper (*Turkestanskia Viedomosti*—'Turkestan News'), and the melancholy monotony of the Muezzin's chant is broken by the cheerful sounds of the bells of the Greek churches, more terrible to Mahomedan ears than the roar of artillery. Popes, soldiers and merchants now move with the proud steps of conquerors through the very streets of Bokhara, where a few years ago the author of this work only dared to venture about chanting Moslem hymns. A Russian hospital and storehouse is established in the once splendid Palace of Timour, whither in the olden times embassies from all the Princes of Asia came to do homage and bring offerings; whither the pround King of Castile himself sent his ambassadors humbly to sue for friendship, and where the descendants of the Turanians came with pious reverence to touch with their foreheads the 'blue stone,' the pedestal of Timour's throne." Who, after reading Vambéry's account of the brutal cruelties practised by the Emir of Bokhara, can wish that in a contest between Bokhara and Russia Bokhara should have prevailed?

Had the Khan of Bokhara been only a little less barbarous than he actually was, the influence of England might, nearly half a century ago, have been brought to bear upon the Khanates of Bokhara, Khokand, and Khiva. The Emperor Nicholas proposed in 1844 that these Khanates should be left independent and untouched by the Russians on the understanding that Russia and England worked together in the Eastern question. Six years earlier the English project in connection with these States had been that they should be induced to form an alliance in order to resist all attacks from Russia. With this view Captain Abbott and Captain Shakespear were sent to Khiva, Colonel Stoddart to Bokhara, and Captain Conolly to Kokhand. " Eagerly," writes Sir John Kaye, in his admirable *" History of the War in Afghanistan,"* " did Arthur Conolly grasp the idea of this Kokhand mission. He was a man of an earnest, impulsive nature, running over with the purest feelings of benevolence, and glowing with the most intense longings after the civilization and evangelization of the human race. He believed that the great Central Asia movement was designed by Providence to break down the huge walls which begirt the shining East, and to substitute

s

civilization, liberty, and peace for barbarism, slavery and strife. He was a visionary, but one of the noblest order; and when he looked out beyond the great barrier of the Hindu-Kush, traversed in imagination the deserts of Merv, and visited the barbarous courts of the Khans of Khiva, Khokand, and Bokhara, he never doubted for a moment that the mission which he was about to undertake was one of the highest with which a Christian officer could be entrusted. 'I feel very confident,' he wrote to a friend, 'about all our policy in Central Asia; for I think that the designs of our Government here are honest, and that they will work with a blessing from God, who seems now to be breaking up all the barriers of the long-closed East, for the introduction of Christian knowledge and peace. It is deeply interesting to watch the effects that are being produced by the exertions of the European powers, some selfish and contrary; others still selfish, but qualified with peace and generosity; all made instrumental to good. See the French in Africa; the English, Austrians, and Russians on the Bosphorous, forcing the Turks to be European under a shadow of Mahomedanism, and providing for the peaceful settlement of the fairest and most sacred countries in the world.'"

Abbott and Shakespear succeeded in at least one part of their mission; they procured the liberation of the Russians kept captive at Khiva, who were conducted to Orenburg under Captain Shakespear's care. Stoddart, however, at Bokhara, after being insulted and tortured in every possible manner, was put to death ; and the enthusiastic Conolly, on reaching Bokhara, met with the same fate.

It must be added that, Butenef, a Russian who arrived at Bokhara towards the close of Stoddart's captivity, did his best to save both the Englishmen. His efforts were all in vain.

CHAPTER XII.

PROJECTS FOR THE INVASION OF INDIA.

As long as Russia was occupied with operations against the Khanates, the possibility of a Russian advance to India through Balkh and Cabul seems alone to have been thought of. Such was the case when the Earl of Clarendon, at his interview with Prince Gortschakoff, at Heidelberg in 1869, commenced the negotiations which, four years afterwards, ended in what at the time was considered a satisfactory (though incomplete) arrangement in regard to the Afghan boundary. The Russians, he observed, already in possession of Samarcand, with Bokhara in their power, and constantly advancing in the direction of Afghanistan, might soon be expected in the vicinity of the Hindu-Kush, whence "the British possessions might be viewed as a traveller on the summit of Simplon might survey the plains of Italy;" so that "measures for our own protection might then become necessary." Thus, in the now historical conversation between the two Ministers, an English statesman saw danger where danger is no longer seen—not because it has ceased to exist, but because it has been overshadowed by a greater peril.

After the subjection of the three Khanates of Khokand, Bokhara, and Khiva, Russia began to deal seriously with the Turcoman tribes, in occupation of the deserts which barred her way from the Caspian to Herat; and the Russian route of progress towards India to which attention is now chiefly directed is the one through Herat and Candahar.

But there is a third route of invasion which may one day be employed in conjunction with the two others. The late Lieutenant Hayward was convinced that India might, without much difficulty, be entered from Eastern Turkestan. "An army," he wrote, "attempting a passage across the mountains from Eastern Turkestan to India would have no great impediment to encounter until it had entered the deeper defiles of the lower Himalayas. . . . . A portion of the line intervening between the crest of the Karakorum range and the plains of Turkestan is quite practicable; and as, in all human probability, it is here that the Russian and the Indian Empires will first come into contact, and the frontiers run conterminous, this fact is deserving of special consideration."

Meanwhile it should not be forgotten that the great historical route for invaders advancing towards India from Central Asia has been the one through Herat and Candahar. This was the actual route of Gerighis Khan, Timour, Baber, and, in the last century, Nadir Shah; the proposed route of the Emperors Paul and Alexander I. This, too, was the route recommended by General Khruleff and General Duhamel at the time of the Crimean war, and by General Skobeleff—conjointly with an advance through the Bamian pass and Cabul—when the last war waged by Russia against Turkey was on the point of breaking out.

GENERAL KHRULEFF'S PROJECT (1855).

"The important question of shaking the rule of the English to its foundations, and of inciting the subject races to an attempt to gain their freedom, may be determined," wrote General Khruleff in 1855, just before the termination of the war in the Crimea, "by the despatch of a corps of thirty thousand men to Candahar. The essential conditions, however, are, in the first place, the perfect neutrality of Persia and the co-operation of Afghanistan in the war." After showing how the friendship of Persia may be secured, he continues as follows:—

"The Afghans applied to Russia in 1837 and 1838 for protection against the English; they will be gratified at our endeavour to overthrow the English rule; their detestation of the English is yet alive. If the English anticipate us and invade Afghanistan to check our influence, our plan can be carried into effect all the sooner. There will then be a popular outbreak before our appearance. The English cannot introduce a large army into that mountainous country. Death will face them in every defile, as was the case in their war with the Afghans. If the English resolve upon a defensive war in their Indian dominions, then our presence in Afghanistan will promote the rising of the Indians against the hated English rule. A movement of troops will be difficult for the English."

The precautions which General Khruleff recommends in view of possible attacks from the Khivans and from the Turcoman tribes would now no longer be necessary; and all that he says on that head may be passed over.

As to the line of march and the feeding of the troops, he writes :—

"The road from Ak-Kala to Candahar offers no difficulties. It is practicable for artillery and for a commissariat train; water, rice, barley, and sheep can be procured in plenty. The grazing land is good. The expeditions of Shah Mahomed have shown that some tens of thousands of soldiers totally unprovided for have found provisions on the road through Bujnurd, Kuchan, Meshed, and Herat. Captain Blaremberg, of our own service, participated in one of these campaigns, and in the siege of Herat, when it was defended by Lieut. Pottinger, of the English Army. The siege of Herat was in 1838. From Meshed to Herat we should find easy means of transport, on account of the great concentration of caravans at Meshed. The country around Herat is famous for its fertility. From Ak-Kala the troops would reach Herat in thirty-five days, marching twenty-five versts [from sixteen to seventeen miles] per day. The march of the English troops into Afghanistan showed that, whilst coming as enemies, their army was supplied with forage by the natives. We may be perfectly sure that we should encounter no difficulty in the matter of supplies. The road from

Herat to Candahar, the gate of India, is known to us. Captain Vitkievitch was sent to Cabul by General Simonitch, our envoy in Persia. Having secured the neutrality of Persia, and having made ourselves secure on the side of Khiva, Bokhara, and Khokand [Russia, by the subjection of Khiva, Bokhara, and Khokand, has made herself quite secure on this side] we could at once march a force of 30,000 men to Candahar, sending an embassy from thence to Cabul, which would finally dispose the natives in our favour, and raise our influence over that of the English.

"While stating my plan" (continues General Khruleff) " I am deeply penetrated with a conviction of the possibility of carrying it into execution; and of this the English are better assured than we are. A numerous force would be embarrassing; we should endeavour to raise a native force; our own should form the reserve. We are bound to instruct the population in our methods of offering opposition to the oppression of the English, whose force in India consists of only twenty-five thousand European troops. The army of India, according to Major Everest, consisting of three hundred thousand men, is dispersed over an extent of one million and seventy-six thousand, five hundred and ninety English miles, and is called upon to guard a frontier of seven hundred and seven geographical miles, being at the same time commanded by only seven thousand three hundred and forty-three European officers, which was the establishment in 1847. There have been many instances in which these troops have fled before compact masses of England's native foes, when the officers were killed. The entrance of a long-desired corps of thirty thousand men into Afghanistan will excite the national antipathy of the Afghans to the English, and will shake the power of the English in India.

"We may make compromises" (concludes General Khruleff) "with our other foes; but England's bearing towards us, which tends to the weakening of our power, does not justify us in leaving her at peace. We must free the people who are the sources of her wealth, and prove to the world the might of the Russian Czar."

GENERAL DUHAMEL'S PROJECT.

This project was drawn up and submitted to the Emperor Nicholas in 1854, at the beginning of the Crimean War, by General Duhamel, who succeeded Count Simonitch as Minister in Persia, when the latter, after the failure of the Russo-Persian siege of Herat, had been withdrawn. It is the same, in principle, as the project by General Khruleff, which was laid before the Emperor Nicholas when the war was drawing to a conclusion.

" When, towards the close of the last century, an army corps was quartered on the Eastern frontiers by order of the Emperor Paul, with a design on India, the English nation, although not certain of the fact, was greatly startled by the intelligence. Since then English writers have never ceased to point out in different ways the danger of a Russian invasion of India, and their Parliament has often discussed the question. The present war, which is declared to the knife, imposes upon Russia the duty of showing how she can attack England in her only vulnerable point, in India, and thus force her to assemble so great a force in Asia as to weaken her action in Europe. History teaches us that nearly all the Powers which conquered India found their way to it through Central Asia and Persia, and that the roads by which Alexander the Great, Genghis Khan, Amerlane, Sultan Baber, and, lastly, Nadir Shah, broke into India are now also open ; they pass through Khorassan and Afghanistan, whether they lead from Persia or from the Oxus. The towns of Candahar and Cabul are the gates of the Indies.

"1. The first road leads from Orenburg over the table land of Ursturt to Khiva, and further on through Merv, Herat, Candahar to Cabul.

"2. The second route goes from Orsk or Orenburg to the fortress of Aralsk, and thence to the cities of Bokhara, Balkh Kalum, and Cabul.

"3. The third starts from Orsk or Troitzk, goes through Aralsk and Ak-Meshed to Tashkend, or leads direct through to Petropawlowsk, and, further, to Kokhand, Kalum, Bamian, and Cabul.

"4. The fourth is from Astrakhan by water to Astrabad, and thence through Redushan, or Shahnid to Meshed, Herat, Candahar, and Cabul.

"5. The fifth, and last road, leads from Dshuelfa, on the river Araxes, to Tabris, Teheran, Meshed, Herat, Candahar, and Cabul.

"The three first roads lead through the desert in its fullest width; and here, even if the oasis of Khiva and that of Bokhara were made use of, it would need thousands of camels to transport provisions for the troops. The fourth and fifth roads lead through a country which is not crossed by deserts, and which is in some parts very fertile and inhabited by energetic tribes. They do not lead over any such inaccessible points as those in the Hindu-Kush mountains; neither is one stopped on the way by an impassable river, as, for instance, the Oxus, between Bokhara and Balkh. When once the necessary transports are on the Caspian Sea and ready for use, then the road from Astrakhan to Astrabad is preferable to all others, for the distance is the shortest. Once in Astrabad, a footing in Khorassan would be easy, and the remaining distance to Cabul is only 1870 versts. The infantry, artillery, and ammunition would be shipped over the Caspian Sea, whilst the cavalry and ammunition train would travel from Circassia through Persia. For it would be a dangerous march through Turkestan, having to combat the Khans and their tribes, who, when repulsed, would again attack in the rear, and thus cut off communication. Comparatively easy, however, would be the march through half-civilized Persia, which is already so bound by treaties that it is incapable of any serious resistance, and is, moreover, threatened from all sides (especially from Circassia), and so rendered powerless. What more then remains to be desired? Any active co-operation on the part of the Persians involves active co-operation on the part of Afghanistan on account of the deadly animosity which exists between the two; and this is just the *conditio sine quâ non* of an attack upon India. Of course, England would not be behindhand in taking steps to prevent all this; but, even had she time and means for sending an expedition to the Persian gulf, taking possession of Karak and Binder-Bushirs, or inciting the South Persian tribes to rebellion, it would be of little avail should Russia guarantee to the Shah his throne and possessions; still less, should she promise the restoration of the Turkish districts of Bagdad, Kerseldi, and a part of Kurdistan, and thereby kindle a war between Persia and Turkey. The road through Persia is, therefore, for many reasons preferable to those through Turkestan.

" There are three roads leading from Afghanistan to India.

" 1. From Cabul, through Jellahabad and Peshawur to Attok.

" 2. From Ghazna to Dera Ismael Khan.

" 3. From Candahar, through Quetta and Dadur to Shikarpur.

"These three roads lead through passes which are easy to defend, but which are all more exposed to a successful attack from the west than from the east. The best, shortest, and healthiest route is the first, although in 1839 the English chose the third. From Attok lies an easier road to Lahore and Delhi, the main points of attack. The choice of this route would create a rebellion in the very heart of England's possessions, and cause all the Mahomedan tribes to rise against her. In this direction lies, for the Afghans, the most tempting prospect of booty and acquisition of territory. Should this be the means also of winning over the Sikhs, so much the better; but the Afghan alliance is of the greatest importance. This once accomplished, all is won; for we do not invade India with a view to making conquests, but to overthrow the English rule—or at least to weaken English power. In order to effect this only a small army is needed, to form the kernel of the invasion round which all the conquered tribes would cluster, and which might be gradually reduced as a general rising caused the attacking forces to swell."

GENERAL SKOBELEFF'S PROJECT (1877).

The following project by the late General Skobeleff was published in the Russian "*Monthly Historical Review*" for December, 1883. It was addressed by

General Skobeleff, in January, 1877, from Khokand, to an intimate friend; and it was afterwards found among the papers of the late Prince Cherkaski :—

"I am thoroughly convinced that we need not anticipate anything of a serious nature from the natives of Turkestan in the event of a war with Turkey. Therefore if we wage war with Turkey alone, and if the idea of the aggressive attitude which would determine the importance of Turkestan, in case of a war with England, has not yet ripened in our higher spheres, it would be insufferable to remain here in time of war.

"One of the objects of this letter is to remind you of my recent independent action in warfare. But its main purport is to express to you candidly my opinion that it is proper, as it is possible, to launch an expedition from Turkestan in the event of a breach with England, in order to promote the triumph and greatness of Russia.

"The aim I here indicate is one of world wide significance. No Russian patriot, recognizing the possibility of a successful achievement of the purpose, and placed by destiny in a position to guide the operation, can hesitate to point out the immense resources which, I will permit myself to say, our

Government has accidentally accumulated on this frontier, and by means of which, with adequate resolution and with timely preparation, it is possible, not only to strike an effective blow at England in India, but also to crush her in Europe. All this, I repeat, can be done while we retain full possession of the Turkestan province, rendering it perfectly secure as a base of operations. In this I most firmly believe, having abundant proofs of our power and influence, so long as we act in Asia more than anywhere else up to this maxim: 'Waste no words where you may exercise your authority.'

"Fortified by an obligation to do my duty at a most trying time for Russia, I submitted a Note on the 27th December 1876 to the Governor-General, and I wrote to my uncle Alexander; now I address you, fearless of the consequences to myself, and praying to God that due attention, in proper quarters, may be given to that powerful aggressive force which we wield in Central Asia.

"I was appointed to the command of the forces in the Namangan district in the month of September 1875, pending the arrival of reinforcements which were expected from Russia in the spring of 1876. The condition of affairs on our frontier was at that time exceedingly serious and very unfavourable to us; so much so that the force entrusted with the defence of the district was composed of 18 companies, and 8 sotnias of Cossacks, with 14 field guns, irrespective of ordnance for defensive works. The gravity of the situation under which the troops under my command were placed became at once obvious on the withdrawal of the main body to Hodjend on the 16th November 1875.

"The enemy hurled themselves *en masse* on the 23rd October against the unfinished fortifications at Namangan, and from that time we had incessant engagements with them. The result of this was the storming of Namangan, and the clearing of the district of all insurgents. Supplies being then secured, we assumed the offensive, and routed the whole of the Khokand army of 40,000 men at Balykchi on the 12th November, 1875. After a series of more or less sanguinary actions, the Namangan detachment stormed Andijan for the second time on the 8th of January 1876, scattered the remaining forces of the war party at Assaké, compelled the leader Abdur Rahman Avtobachi, to surrender himself, and after a six months' campaign laid the entire Khanate of Khokand at the feet of His Imperial Majesty.

"This happened one year ago, and about that time I was appointed Military-Governor of the Ferghana region.

"The region abounded with disturbing elements. With a view to its pacification I marched the troops to the Alai, where, being animated by pacific objects, I acted accordingly. The Alai campaign did not cost Russia a single drop of blood, the rebels being forced to abandon their inaccessible strongholds by purely strategic marches. Thus, I imagine, I fulfilled in the highest degree the desire of His Majesty who cherishes the blood of his subjects.

"You yourself have had occasion to see what was effected administratively from the general order issued by the Governor-General.

"It is not for me at such a period to dispose of my own self. The authorities are better able to say where I can be most advantageously employed. In every case I now unbosom myself to you, and make known to you my desire to join the army in the field at any moment and in any capacity. I am all the less in a position to apply for leave to quit this region, because I firmly believe in its aggressive power as an agent for the solution of the Eastern question.

"It has been frequently said that from Central Asia Russia can threaten the British rule in India, and that it is therefore absolutely necessary for England at this juncture to check the advance of the Russian troops in Turkestan.

"If we look around us, we shall find that our position in Turkestan is indeed most formidable, and that the apprehensions of the English are not groundless. We have established a strong base in Central Asia, with an army of about 40,000 men, from which we shall always be able to detach a force of not less than 10,000 or 12,000 men for operations outside the limits of the province; at the same time we may trust implicitly in the fidelity of our subjects, for even now there is not the slightest indication of any combination of the Mahomedans of Turkey with those of Central Asia.

"By reinforcing the troops in Turkestan, say with six companies from Western Siberia, with as many Siberian Cossacks as could be spared, with one battery, and with three regiments of Cossacks from Orenburg, we might organize a column of about 14,000 or 15,000 men.

"Such a column thrown across the Hindu-Kush could effect a great deal.

"The position of the English in India has been said to be precarious by every one who has studied the question. It has been stated that the English tenure of India is by the sword alone; that the number of European troops in India is not more than sufficient to keep order in the country, and that the Native army is not to be trusted.

"Every one referring to the question of a Russian invasion of India has declared that an approach to the frontier would be enough to raise a rebellion.

"It may be said that an enterprise against the English in India is a matter of great risk; that it might end disastrously for the Russian force. I do consider, and we should not close our eyes to the fact, that the enterprise would indeed be a risky one. We should, however, bear in mind that if we were successful we should entirely demolish the British Empire in India; and the effect of this in England cannot be calculated beforehand. Competent English authorities admit that an overthrow on the frontiers of India might even produce a social revolution in England, because for the last 20 years England has been tied closer than ever to her Indian possessions by reasons and phenomena (including an incapacity for war) identical with those of France. In a word, the downfall of the British supremacy in India would be the beginning of the downfall of England.

"Should our venture not result in complete success, *i.e.,* should a rebellion fail to break out in India; and should we fail to cross the frontier, we should at all events compel the English to keep the whole of their Indian Army in Hindustan and render it impossible for them to spare any portion of it for service in Europe; they would indeed find themselves obliged to transport some of their forces from Europe to India. In short we could, to a great extent, paralyse the land forces of England as regards either a European war or the selection of a new theatre of war, from the Persian Gulf by Tabriz to Tiflis in connection with the armies of Turkey and Persia: an idea which has been entertained by English Officers since the Crimean war.

"The necessity of making Turkestan participate in forthcoming events is rendered necessary by the circumstance that in the event of the termination of a war in any way unfavourable to us, we should most certainly have to evacuate the Turkestan province or limit our authority in that region. But should we be beaten both in Europe and Asia, we should have proved even by our disastrous enterprise the formidable nature of our position in Central Asia ; and, being reduced by necessity to conclude a humiliating treaty, Russia might get off at the price of Turkestan, which would have risen in value.

" There can be no comparison between the risk we run in making a demonstration against British India and the enormous advantages which we should gain in the event of the success of such a demonstration.

" The gigantic difference in the results of a successful issue to us and to our enemies is of itself enough to urge us boldly onwards.

" On the proclamation of war with England, we should begin at once in Turkestan by despatching a Mission to Cabul and form a column in Samarcand (which, for effect, I should call an army), composed of 10 battalions, 14 sotnias, and 40 guns, making a total of 10,000 to 12,000 men ; this should positively be the minimum of our aggressive force.

" The object of the Mission should be to draw Shir Ali into an alliance with us, and to open relations with the disaffected natives of India ; and in order to secure the success of these negotiations, the column should be pushed through Bamian to Cabul. If it be found that Shir Ali adheres to the English (which is not very probable, because he did not accept the invitation to be present among other vassals on the occasion of the proclamation of the title of Empress of India and Delhi, and even expressed his annoyance at the receipt of the invitation), a claimant to the throne should be put forward in the person of Abdur-Rahman-Khan, who is residing in Samarcand; by which means internal dissensions might be brought about in Afghanistan, while on the other hand Persia might be conveniently urged to renew her claims to Herat. By turning Persia's attention to Afghanistan, we should divert her military forces from the Caucasus. The march of the Persian troops to Herat would call into requisition all the supplies and means of transport of the country, and this would most effectually paralyse any English plan of an advance from the Persian gulf to Tiflis.

" The invading column having left Samarcand, another should be at once formed in that place of two battalions of infantry, and 16 sotnias of Cossacks, with one battery of artillery for the purpose of occupying points along our line of communication and for general service in the rear.

" Without entering into details, I would divide the campaign into two periods. The first period should be one of extremely rapid action, of diplomatic negotiation with Afghanistan, supported by an advance of the column to Cabul. The second period, commencing with the occupation of Cabul, should be a waiting period, during which we should maintain relations with the disaffected elements in India, giving them the means to express themselves in the way best calculated to serve our interests (the principle reason of the failure of the Mutiny in 1857 was want of organization on the part of the rebels), and finally—as also chiefly—to organize masses of Asiatic cavalry which, to a cry of blood and booty, might be launched into India, as the vanguard; thus renewing the times of Timur.

"The further operations of the Russian column from Cabul cannot be sketched in this plan of campaign. At best the operations might terminate in the presence of the Russian banners at Benares; at worst, the column would retire with honour to Herat, meeting a force despatched from the Caucasus, which should consist of several battalions, with 6 guns to every 1,000 men. An Asiatic force, especially the Turcomans, are not formidable in the open field; and even the invincible English army would thaw away* very considerably in marching to

* "The acclimatized Russian troops are undoubtedly better qualified than English soldiers to endure the hardship of a Central Asian campaign."—"*History of the War in Afghanistan,*" by J. W. Kaye.

Herat. Nor are the English in a position to march a body of more than 25,000 men beyond the frontier of India, and of these a large number would have to be told off along the line of communication. It is at the same time not to be forgotten that the Turkestan province would be on the flank of the enemy's line of communication, and that our resources would increase as we drew nearer to the Caspian.

"I have already said that this enterprise would be attended with risk. But it would be justified by the greatness of the object in view and by the immeasurable vastness of its possible results. From the standpoint of these results there can be for Russia no question as to risk, and, as to Turkestan, it is not worth mentioning.

"From the troops who should be so fortunate as to be selected for this campaign, we should expect something even more than self-sacrifice in the highest sense of the word as it is understood by military men.

"Upon crossing the Hindu-Kush the column should, in my opinion, be so managed that every man might feel that he had come to Afghanistan to conquer or to die ; that each man might know that the Emperor required even his death. We should not be reproached for leaving our standards in the hands of the enemy if not a single Russian warrior remained alive beyond the Hindu-Kush.

"Such a feeling and such a determination can, in my opinion, be based only on the sentiment commonly cherished by every soldier in the army, of an unswerving and boundless love for and devotion to his monarch. The difficulty of exalting the spirit of the column to a pitch corresponding with the nature of the enterprise, could best be met by attaching one of the Emperor's sons, who at the proper time might tell the troops what was expected of them by the Czar and by their country. I am perfectly assured that this column, favoured by the presence of one of His Majesty's sons, would do wonders, and would in no case disgrace the Russian name.

" During the course of their 10 years' experience in this region, the Turkestan troops have become trained to a systematic mode of military operations founded on a knowledge of local conditions, of the nature of their opponents, but principally on a consciousness of their readiness at any time to take the field. All this enables them to plan operations in the future in accordance with the military resources of Turkestan. If we continue to handle our troops as they have hitherto been handled we shall not meet with any insurmountable obstacles in Central Asia.

"Asiatic crowds may inconvenience us, but they cannot hinder us in the accomplishment of our designs. We have reached the stage in which, with judicious and systematic action,—possessing artillery and ammunition beyond the proportions needed in European warfare,—we can strike with effect in the open field and in the mountains. We can now do this, I repeat, without sustaining any loss, being thoroughly versed in military operations. In a word, with our present experience, with our excellent, and, in my opinion, sufficiently numerous troops, and with the resources which we command, there is no Asia capable of preventing us from carrying out the broadest strategical designs which we might conceive.

"Our policy of the last ten years has raised the significance of Russia in the world. In the opinion of the English, as also of the Asiatics, there are no limits to the grand operations of our Government. The security of our position rests mainly upon the effect of this belief. I was greatly struck by an observation by Colonel Cory, in his '*Shadows of Coming Events; or, the Eastern Menace,*' to the effect that he could not picture to his imagination a power in Turkestan otherwise than in connection with Russia by a direct line of rail between Chardjui, on the Oxus, and Moscow. The Asiatics believe, up to the present moment, that the Russians spit fire when they make a rush with a cheer.

"A knowledge of this region, and of its resources, leads inevitably to the conclusion that our presence in Turkestan, in pursuance of Russian interests, is justifiable solely on the ground of an endeavour to solve the Eastern question in our own favour from this quarter. Otherwise the hide is not worth the tanning, and all the money sunk in Turkestan is lost. We should beware lest we prove to our enemies, by inaction in Asia at a critical moment in the West, how aimless have been our annexations; this, too, would most certainly involve a loss of influence, and would necessitate in the future a still larger unproductive outlay. I repeat that, with a force of 40,000 men as a minimum, dexterously handled, we might not only keep in restraint all Turkestan, Kashgar, and Bokhara combined in hostilities against us, but even—and I say it boldly—evacuate Turkestan and re-conquer it.

"In case of need we could increase our forces here by 6 regiments of mounted Siberian Cossacks (36 sotnias), several companies from Western Siberia (6 sotnias), 1 battery (8 guns) of artillery, and perhaps 3 regiments (18 sotnias) from Orenburg.

"We must bear in mind that in despatching say from 16,000 to 20,000 men across the Hindu-Kush with a corresponding force of artillery, of which we have no lack in Turkestan, being reinforced as above, we should still have 31,000 men left to garrison the province; and this, too, without drawing on the Oxus detachment (2 battalions, 4 sotnias, and 2 field guns), and without taking into account the troops in the Trans-Caspian region.

"We have doubtless a great deal more to go through in the future in Central Asia. But the present generation of Mahomedans born under the ægis of Russian law has first to grow up into manhood; ere that time an entire class of influential natives well acquainted with us, and recognising the causes of our power and of our success, will spring up. The notorious Nana Sahib was educated among Europeans and was received in the best English society, and it was only on that account that he was such a terror to the English. We have as yet no such elements in our midst, and in this circumstance lies one of our positive advantages over the English. When political events in the West are coming to a crisis this important consideration, coupled with many others, should urge us to derive all the benefit out of Turkestan which that province is capable of yielding us.

"'In Asia, when triumphs cease difficulties commence.' *

"This is undoubtedly true. In a political sense we are now living in a period of triumphs. Let us profit by it.

"You see how much I expect from our might in Central Asia. Having for some considerable time shared with the Turkestan forces in the hardships of campaigning, I do not wish to exchange active service here for any other elsewhere. I could not, however, remain inactive in this place while the greater part of our army was shedding its blood in the country's cause in the West. That is why I

---

* Correspondence of the Duke of Wellington with Lord Auckland, 1839.

beg you again to bear me in mind in the event of a declaration of war.

"Michael Skobeleff.

"P.S.—I enclose some general orders to our troops in Ferghana, in illustration of our mode of life here. Peruse them, and give me your opinion upon them.

"I have just received the *Golos* of the 29th December 1876, and I observe from the leading article in it that 'a declaration of war by Russia against the Ottoman Porte is a desideratum of our enemies,' that 'Europe has entangled the question, and trusts to Russia's impatience,' and further, that 'the circumstances are such that a thorough and quick solution of the question is perfectly impossible.'

"To us, who are acquainted with our own military resources in Asia, the Eastern question, of which the solution should be fearful only to the foes of Russia, presents itself otherwise.

"So long ago as in the third decade of the present century, General Field Marshal Count Moltke dwelt on the impossibility of achieving rapid results in European Turkey, and considered that it would be a matter of great difficulty to conduct a war in that country without the aid of a powerful fleet and an absolute mastery of the Black Sea. Field Marshal Prince Varshafski gave it as his opinion in 1829 that aggressive operations in Asia would be of but little importance, seeing that there was no great and all-determining point of attack, although he considered the trade routes connecting Bagdad with Scutari the best objectives in this respect. The construction of the Suez Canal has, however, deprived even this line of all significance.

"One might for this reason positively assert that, however successfully we might conduct a campaign in European and in Asiatic Turkey, yet we should vainly seek there for a solution of the Eastern question. A sincere behaviour on the part of England, in conformity with the interests of our Government, in so far as I comprehend the question, might, indeed, lead to the satisfaction of our legitimate demands. Therefore I imagine we should not have two opinions on the matter of a war with England. Without a formal declaration of war, England might still be at war with us by sending officers to the Turkish army and by helping Turkey with supplies.

"Would it not be best to avail ourselves of our strong strategical position in Central Asia, of our better acquaintance with the communications in and resources of Central Asia, in order to strike a deadly blow at our real enemies in the doubtful event of the evidence of our determination to operate against their most vulnerable point being alone insufficient to make them pliant?

"The condition of affairs is apparently grave; therefore, while resolving to maintain only a defensive attitude on the Danube and in Asiatic Turkey, we might satisfy ourselves with landing 30,000 men at Astrabad to march to Cabul, in conjunction with the Turkestan troops. By this means we should free the Russian army in Europe and in Asia Minor from those embarrassments against which it fights, periodically, without success, several times in the course of every century.

"It is not for me to say how we are to defend the Caucasus against a Turkish invasion, nor how long the army of the Danube might remain in a purely defensive attitude in the midst of the helpless Christian population of Turkey, but it is my positive opinion that,—

"1. If under the existing circumstances of the extent of the British authority in India the invasion of India with a corps of 18,000 men is a possibility and a desirability, although attended with risk, an invasion with a force of 50,000 men is perfectly free from all risk.

" 2. We command on the Caspian from the early spring the means to concentrate with rapidity a force of 30,000 men at Astrabad fully provided for.

" 3. A large force can easily march from Astrabad to Herat and to Cabul. By exercising a political pressure on Persia, we might draw all our supplies from Khorassan.

"4. The Turkestan military district, reinforced with six regiments of Siberian Cossacks, three regiments or Orenburg Cossacks, six companies of infantry, and one battery of artillery from Western Siberia (these troops might reach Taskhend by spring time), could send a body of 18,000 men with artillery to Cabul.

" 5. The troops can be marched from Samarcand to the Hindu-Kush, and can be further marched from Khullum through Haibuk, Kurram, and Bamian and across the Kora-Kotul, Dendan-Shiken, Ak-Robat, Kalui, Hadjikhak, and Unai passes, into the valley of Cabul-Daria. Although artillery has been taken over the above-named passes without extra appliances, I have nevertheless given my attention to this subject with the view of facilitating the passage of guns.

"I am now in a position to state that we have an easy method of transporting guns; yesterday a 4-pounder was slung under a newly-contrived cart, and a trial with it was successfully made. On the merits of this mode of transport we can pronounce only in February next after practical experience; a trial is to be made with two guns over the snow-covered mountains in this region.

"6. Shir-Ali, the successor of Dost Mahommed, must necessarily contemplate the recovery of Peshawer, and it is not difficult to raise all Asia against India to a cry of 'blood and booty.'

"7. Shir-Ali is at present dissatisfied with the English.

"8. There are barely more than 60,000 British soldiers in India at present, with a corresponding force of artillery, and the Native army is more a menace than a support to the rulers of India.

"9. The very appearance of even a small force on the Indian frontier is enough to raise a rebellion in India, and to ensure the overthrow of the British dominion.

"All this should, in my mind, be taken into serious consideration at the present moment.

"Khokand, 27th January, 1877."

The following comments on the late General Skobeleff's Letter are made by the Editor of the *"Historical Review"*:—

"Six years have rolled away since the above words rang out, since the patriot wrote that when it is a question of the welfare of Russia there can be no question of risk, for Russian soldiers beyond the Hindu-Kush will know, if needs be, how to die to the last man. Six years have elapsed, years pregnant with so much! The war in which the late General so modestly begged to be allowed to participate was declared: the campaign was brilliantly gained by the army, but lost by diplomacy. An embassy under General Stolietoff was sent to Shir-Ali, and it returned, we know how from Dr. Yavorski's book. The brilliant Akhal-Téké campaign improved the condition of our Turkestan frontier. Much else has changed during the last six years. Many actors in the political arena have disappeared, together with Skobeleff himself. And the operations of the English in Egypt, with their practical sovereignty over that country, have materially altered the aspect of the Eastern question, and in military respects have changed its character. Nor have the English successes in Afghanistan failed to affect the problems of our future policy in Turkestan. All this has tended to change the historical significance of the interminable Eastern question, both from the English and Russian points of view.

"We cannot tell whether the author of the above letter would have held to his opinions if he had lived till now; whether he would still have considered that the Achilles' heel of the British power is in India, that the Gordian knot of the Eastern question is to be cut there after the fashion of Timur, in order that Russia may gain possession of the gateway to her own Black Sea. We can receive no direct answer to these inquiries; the heart of the patriot has ceased to beat; his great mind works for us no more. One thing, however, is certain, that others equally large-minded and penetrating will ever find a simple and ready solution for every question at the time of necessary action. They will not, of course, refer to historical characters like Skobeleff for guidance in matters of detail, which must be governed by changing circumstances, but they will nevertheless find much that is worthy of emulation in his manner of acting with boldness, in the strength of his convictions, in the soundness and fearlessness of his deductions. It is in this sense that the document which we publish here is historically instructive."

THE END.

www.ingramcontent.com/pod-product-compliance
Lightning Source LLC
Chambersburg PA
CBHW032047230426
43672CB00009B/1501